2021 Year of Tarot

2021 Year of Tarot

Connect with your deck through a year of exercises & spreads

D.E. Luet

ALL RIGHTS RESERVED.

COPYRIGHT © 2020 BY DANIELLE LUET

WWW.AWITCHALONESHOP.COM

NO PART OF THIS BOOK MAY BE REPRODUCED OR TRANSMITTED IN ANY FORM OR BY ANY MEANS, ELECTRONIC OR MECHANICAL, INCLUDING PHOTOCOPYING, RECORDING, OR BY ANY INFORMATION STORAGE OR RETRIEVAL SYSTEM, WITHOUT PERMISSION IN WRITING FROM THE PUBLISHER.

PUBLISHER: A WITCH ALONE PUBLISHING

ANY UNAUTHORIZED USE, SHARING, REPRODUCTION, OR DISTRIBUTION OF THESE MATERIALS BY ANY MEANS, ELECTRONIC, MECHANICAL, OR OTHERWISE IS STRICTLY PROHIBITED. NO PORTION OF THESE MATERIALS MAY BE REPRODUCED IN ANY MANNER WHATSOEVER, WITHOUT THE EXPRESS WRITTEN CONSENT OF THE PUBLISHER.

ISBN (PAPERBACK): 978-1-7773189-3-2

ISBN (HARDCOVER): 978-1-7773189-5-6

ISBN (EBOOK): 978-1-7773189-4-9

DISCLAIMER: THE MATERIAL FOUND IN THIS BOOK IS FOR INTROSPECTIVE PRACTICES ONLY. THE AUTHOR IS NOT A CERTIFIED THERAPIST AND THE ADVICE/SPREADS YOU FIND IN THIS BOOK SHOULD NOT BE USED IN REPLACEMENT OF ANY KIND OF TRADITIONAL THERAPY OR OF MEDICATIONS TAKEN.

ILLUSTRATIONS BY MARA WOODS @GEMINI.CONSORT
ASTROLOGICAL INSIGHT BY ANTHONY PEROTTA @AP_ASTROLOGY

THANK YOU.

If you are afraid of The Fool, how will you know when to begin?

Table of Contents

Preface...1
History...2
Inspiration & Appropriation............................4
Starting Out...6
Picking Your Deck......................................7
Connecting with Your Deck.............................12
Using Your Deck.......................................15
Shuffling & Cutting...................................15
Before you Shuffle....................................16
Types of Shuffling....................................17
Cutting the Deck......................................18
Pulling the Cards.....................................18
Start Small...19
Reading Bigger Spreads................................22
What Affects a Reading?...............................23
Asking Questions & Dealing with Answers...............24
Dealing with a Negative Deck..........................25
Creating your own spreads.............................27
Why create a spread...................................27
Where to start..27
Choosing the spread shape.............................29
Single card pulls.....................................30
2-Card Spreads..31
3-Card Spreads..32
January...33
January new moon......................................39
January full moon.....................................47
February..49
February new moon.....................................57

February full moon.................................63
March...65
March new moon..................................73
March full moon.................................79
April...81
April new moon..................................89
April full moon.................................97
May...99
May new moon...................................107
May full moon..................................113
June...115
June new moon..................................123
June full moon.................................129
July...131
July new moon..................................139
July full moon.................................145
August...149
August new moon................................155
August full moon...............................161
September......................................165
September new moon.............................173
September full moon............................179
October..183
October new moon...............................189
October full moon..............................195
November.......................................199
November new moon..............................205
November full moon.............................211
December.......................................215
December new moon..............................221
December full moon.............................227

Tarot Key; The Suits............................223
Tarot Key; Minor Arcana........................224
Tarot Key: Major Arcana........................237
Zodiacs...239

PREFACE

Tarot fascinated me for a long time, but when others would read for me, I found it so hard to understand how they were getting the messages they were from the cards they were pulling. Nevertheless, their messages always rang true to my situation.

I went through four decks before I finally found one I connected with, and what used to be difficult and frustrating for me, was becoming as easy as breathing.

When trying to find information on how to increase my practice, or my accuracy, I always found the same result: practice. Okay, cool, but **how**. I like instruction. Give me a list that I check things off of when I've completed the necessary task.

That was the inspiration behind this planner, *A Year of Tarot*. Inside you'll find suggestions for daily card pulls, beginning of the week and beginning of the month spreads, spreads for each months full and new moons. You'll also find sections with how to connect to your cards, cleansing them, suggestions for "before first use", tips to create your own spreads, and a full tarot key.

Tarot has become part of my daily life. It is my sounding board. My teacher. My friend. My parent. If you've picked up this planner, I hope it helps you on your way to loving tarot as much as I do.

History

Before beginning on any path, one should really understand where it comes from and how it came to be. Tarot is no exception to this line of thinking and it has an extensive history and it's beginning roots run deeper than many understand.

Like many old and ancient practices, we aren't sure exactly when tarot was first created or what it's original purpose was. There is only speculation about where it originated, why it was first used and how it arrived in the western world.

Tarot cards have been seen in India and the Far East since ancient times, and is suspected that they were brought to Europe by the Knights Templar during and/or after the crusades. Some good to know points about tarot history are:

~16th century magician John Dee used the tarot cards to talk to "angels".

~The origin or calling the deck "tarot" is unknown, but speculated to be named after the Egyptian god Thoth, who ruled over magic and words.

~There is also speculation "tarot" has Hebrew origins or that it is a bastardization of the Hebrew "torah" which is their book of law.

~Tarot as a card game was called "*tarocchi*" or "*taricchino*" which translates to "Trumps"

-The first cards were hand-painted, and the earliest deck we know of is the *Visconti Sforza Tarocchi* cards. These were painted in the 1440's.

-Tarot began as a card game in the west and picked up mystical abilities during the 19th century with the rise of spiritualism. (Ex; The Fox Sisters)

Some of this information you may never have come across, and maybe its common knowledge because you've done your research. Most people that begin on the tarot path, know of the Rider-Waite deck, and you either love it or don't. Something that is important to note with the Rider-Waite deck is that Arthur Waite did not create the deck on his own. It is unsure if he had any creative input into the design of the deck or not, but the real artist and interpreter of the tarot symbols was Pamela Coleman Smith.

Pamela Coleman Smith was an artist of Jamaican decent, orphaned at the age of 21. She created the artwork based on what Arthur Waite dictated to her, and finished the entire set of cards in 6 months at the age of 31. This is a feat all on its own as they would have been hand painted painstakingly, and who knows how many times she would have had to repaint cards because they weren't to Waite's satisfaction.

INSPIRATION & APPROPRIATION

Like many practices we see today, there are roots in other peoples cultures. Many of them disclose that tarot is a closed practice that originated in their culture and no one else should practice it. The Jewish peoples have said that their tarot practice originates from the Kabbalah, and the Romani peoples have said that tarot in general originated with them and is rooted in Asian Shamanism.

Like Hoodoo and Voduo is a specific practice that connects them to their ancestors, the Romani's tarot practice is similar in that their ancestors powers are imbued and speak through, their cards.

What is important to remember is that almost every culture has a form of divination, most of them physically using cards of some kind. (While others use bones or runes.)

Cartomancy as a practice embodies so many types, from tarot to oracle to lenormand and angel decks, and is said to have originated with the Romani and all types of cartomancy are appropriation. I am not about to tell another culture that they are wrong, so I would like you to really consider your decks when choosing them.

Who was the creator? What is their inspiration? Are they using symbols and artwork that are not theirs or that have completely different histories to what their background is? Why are you attracted to their deck in the first place? And the answers to these questions are not wrong or right, but they will give you a level of awareness into the deck you'll be using to speak to higher powers.

I am still of the belief that the cards are another way to speak to the powers that you personally work with, whether that is your deities or your ancestors. If you want something very personal to you, consider making your own deck.

It is important to ask questions and to understand that so many of the practices we have today, in witchcraft or divination or in modern life, more often than not are inspired by something from hundreds of years ago; spiritual or not.

There are many things that we can't argue about, and I wish there was a for sure 100%, non-disputed text that could confirm exactly where tarot began or the first reasons it was created. We don't have that right now, we only have speculations and histories passed down through so many different cultures and ways of life.

Tarot is something that is incredibly personal to the user. A deck that someone loves you may not connect with at all, and the info in these pages may resonate with you or it may not. This is all of my personal understandings, and there is no "right" or "wrong" way to read cards.

Starting Out

First thing I want you to ask yourself, is why are you attracted to tarot? Is it what it could do for you? Is there a deck that has attracted your attention and you don't know why you just *have to have it*? Did you get your cards read and they were so scary accurate you wanted to be able to have that kind of insight at home? These are things you need to be honest with yourself about. If you're simply looking to be able to cheat your way through life and to just *use* your cards, I doubt you'll get the kind of response you're looking for.

"But wait, isn't the whole point to *use* the deck?"

Your tarot deck is not just a tool. It is a friend, a teacher, sometimes it's a bully. It will have its own personality and its own way of giving you answers. As such, your deck(s) should be treated not just as another tool, but as a friend and family. Keep them warm, give them their own cloth and maybe a crystal to keep them happy. If they feel like you are just using them to bs clients or looking for answers about your future without wanting to be introspective, there's a good chance your deck might give you a huge metaphorical middle finger and not cooperate, ever.

You may be asking yourself how a deck of cardboard can have all these personality quirks, but think about the artist that created it. Every unique deck was created with specific energy and intentions by the artist, and most likely you were attracted to a certain deck because your energy saw a friend in the artists energy.

Because of this energy, there will be times when you no longer connect with a deck because where you are in life has changed and so the energy connection has changed. Most of the time, the deck will feel that and will understand that it has given you all that it could and there was a mutual and respectful exchange. (We'll get into breaking up with a deck a little later.)

Picking Your Deck

There are a few opinions on how to acquire a deck. Some people say that you should only be gifted tarot decks, some will tell you that you can totally buy your own deck.

I am of the mind frame that you can pick and buy your own deck, as per the previous section. You are attracted to whatever deck you are because there is an energy connection with the art. The first deck I was ever gifted, I absolutely hated the art, never used it and never connected with it. Because of that, it took me 10 more years before I dared to pick up a tarot deck again.

That being said, I do have the belief that tarot decks are a little more powerful when they have been gifted, and this is coming from personal experience. I had quite the readings with decks I bought myself, but the decks I have been gifted were ones I asked for (birthdays, Yule, etc) so I still had that connection. I think tarot decks are so happy to be given to someone, and my theory on that is that they are usually picking up on the gift givers energy. I love giving people gifts, especially when it's something I know they want, and I am pretty positive a deck would pick up on that and be so excited to make someone happy.

All of my gifted decks have been the friends that always tell you what you need to hear, not what you *want* to hear, and that is a trait I respect in both people and my decks. I want the truth, I don't want it to be sugar coated.

There is also the decision of *which* kind of deck to pick. There are many different varities of decks, but they all fall into three main categories of decks; **tarot, oracle** and **lenormand.**

Tarot cards are the decks that are comprised of 78 cards and split into *Major Arcana* and *Minor Arcana.* (These translate to *Big Secrets* and *Little Secrets.*) The Minor Arcana are organized by suits that correspond to the elements, comprising of 14 cards per suit that range from Ace-10, and the 4 court cards Page, Knight,

Queen and King. The four suits match up each element of Earth, Air, Fire, and Water and depict a linear timeframe of what someone might go through in correspondence with each other the elements.

Earth typically is the suit of finances, career, job, home situation/life and general health.

Air is the suit of wisdom and deals with how you may be looking at a situation, where you may be stunting your own learning or how you work through problems.

Fire is the suit of passions and deal with how driven you are, how you react to problems, and where your passions truly lie in love and in life.

Water is the suit of the emotions and of the heart, and it deals with how you love, how you may view or react in a relationship, and what you place emotional importance on.

Depending on who you talk to, Air and Fire may be switched in their interpretations, so take heed of that when choosing a deck.

The suits are also depicted with symbols similar to a standard playing card deck, and can take the form of any of these symbols;

Earth; coins, pentacles, discs
Air; swords, daggers, athames
Fire; sticks, wands, staffs
Water; cups, chalices, bowls

The Major Arcana depicts qualities seen in all of humanity and in individuals through a life time, from birth to childhood, adult hood and then death. This part of the tarot deck is comprised of 22 cards and are not split into suits, they are simply numbered. You will either see them numbered from 0-21 or 1-22, depending on the artists choice.

The Major Arcana have astrological associations, as laid out below.

0 The Fool	Uranus	11 Justice	Libra
1 The Magician	Mercury	12 The Hanged Man	Neptune
2 The High Priestess	Moon	13 Death	Scorpio
3 The Empress	Venus	14 Temperance	Sagittarius
4 The Emperor	Aries	15 The Devil	Capricorn
5 The Hierophant	Taurus	16 The Tower	Mars
6 The Lovers	Gemini	17 The Star	Aquarius
7 The Chariot	Cancer	18 The Moon	Pisces
8 Strength	Leo	19 The Sun	Sun
9 The Hermit	Virgo	20 Judgement	Pluto
10 The Wheel of Fortune	Jupiter	21 The World	Saturn

Now these associations are argued because some of them don't match up with what planet the zodiac signs are actually associated with, but these associations in the tarot were most likely created before the Zodiac signs were associated with planets.

Next up we have **Oracle** cards. Oracle cards range in deck sizes and don't really have a set organization like tarot cards. Where as tarot cards are always 78 cards, are split into the Major and Minor Arcana and have suits, Oracle cards don't really have a set of rules to follow.

They can depict anything from animals, to nature spirits, to mythological creatures and planets. They can have their meanings written right onto them or they may have just one word. They could have 40 cards or 60 cards, as per the artists discretion.

Oracle cards can usually be used in place of tarot in any kind of spread, and their messages can be a bit clearer depending on your deck, than the tarot is. I tend to see tarot as a more situational deck that will give you a better overview of the situation, but the oracle cards are more introspective and tend to have a more personal touch to their messages. Oracle cards are also much nicer most of the time, where as Tarot is like a smack in the face.

Lenormand decks are decks that look similar to standard playing cards at first glance, but there is less of them and they are usually much smaller than tarot and oracle cards.

This deck consists of 36 cards that seem to have no order or organization. The art on the card is not important to the interpretation but the symbol and the number is. As well as where the card falls in a reading. There is also no rhyme or reason as to why the numbers are paired with the symbols, which can prove to make learning the

Lenormand quite frustrating. These decks are a mix of intuitive reading and of straight facts. It seems to be that what you see is what you get, and that this deck is very straight forward and to the point.

You typically don't deal with reversed cards when using a Lenormand deck. Each card has a specific meaning and there is no room for expressive interpretation, they just mean what they mean either positive or negative.

You can also pair your decks together. Many artists will come out with a tarot and an oracle, and reading them together can give you a more complete picture than just reading one or the other. Even if your deck doesn't have an oracle counterpart, you can still pair two of your favorite decks together and see what happens. (I still suggest shuffling & pulling separately.)

Connecting with Your Deck

The next thing that there is multiple opinions on, is "connecting with your deck." People will tell you that you *have* to do x, y, or z before using your deck or it won't know you. Some people dive right in. I think it's important to do whatever feels right for you and that deck.

I do the same thing with every deck, because it has always worked for me and I feel better doing it, so I'm going to describe to you my practice as well as some other suggestions.

The first thing I do when I get a new deck, is cleanse it. You never know what kind of energies it may have picked up along the way. Even if you bought it directly from the artist, it still changes many hands during shipping to get to you. The best way I do this is with a smoke cleanse from incense. I like to think about the deck and I usually pick an incense I think would go well with it.

After that, I sleep with my new deck under my pillow for 3 nights. My personal theory is that because the subconscious is more open at night, the connection stars at a deeper level. After the 3rd night, I open the deck and go through every card, looking over the artwork and the symbolism. Sometimes I will see a symbol or art work that I remember from a dream during those 3 nights, and more often than not when I look up the meaning, it is very on point for where I am at that moment in time.

I'll then start slow, pulling a card a day for a few weeks, then maybe getting into 3 card spreads, just to give it and me a chance to really get to know each other. I like to use a deck for a month or 2 at least before I ever use it to read for others. Sometimes I won't ever use certain decks to read for others and sometimes I won't ever use a deck to read for myself.

There's nothing wrong with decided to jump right in when you get a new deck though. I do suggest always cleansing before using so that it doesn't get your energy confused with someone else's that might be on it already, but other then that, maybe you connect with your decks better by just using them. If this is your style, I'm going to guess that you're probably a really good person at starting up conversations with strangers and making friends.

Other cleansing and connecting ideas;
~sound cleansing (singing bowl, music)
~meditating with the deck
~sleeping with the deck under your pillow for 7 nights

~giving the deck its own crystal
~giving the deck its own reading cloth

Using Your Deck

There are a few misconceptions about using the tarot, like that it is used to predict the future or that you will be able to see when someone will die. These are not true. The tarot is used to give you insight into yourself and to situations around you or that might arise. It is a tool to provide a better understanding as well as offer advice on how to overcome obstacles you may be faced with in a variety of circumstances. This also can be said about any kind of divination practice and any type of cards.

Shuffling & Cutting

Shuffling is something that again is very personal to the reader. I don't like bending my cards, so I have been a strict over-hand shuffler for so long. I have just decided to rifle shuffling on the corners of my decks to get a more complete shuffling experience. When I read for others, I am pretty strict; they are only allowed to over hand shuffle.

If you have never shuffled tarot cards before, prepare yourself, it is going to feel awkward. The standard playing card size is 2.5' by 3.5', and tarot cards are almost double that coming in at 3.5' by 5.5'. It makes a big difference, especially if you are used to standard playing cards.

I shuffle too fast, and many times I am dropping 2, 3 or 10 cards at a time. There is a mindset that cards that drop out are specifically talking to you, and while I agree with that, I also know that sometimes I am just plain clumsy. After some time you will know when you are being clumsy and when the cards are sending you a specific message.

I have learned that there are a few "rules" that one should *supposedly* follow when reading cards, and these vary in;

~what to do before you shuffle
~how exactly to shuffle
~how to cut
~how to choose cards

Pretty much every aspect of reading has some kind of rule that goes along with it, but as I said before, reading is personal and any rule I've ever come across has never quite sat well with me.

Before You Shuffle

Having a ritual before you begin reading is not necessary, but I would be lying if I didn't say that it did help you get into the mind frame of connecting with your cards and of the energy around you. Like any other ritual, this can be as excessive or as simple as you'd like, from lighting a specific candle or incense, to meditating and ground your energy.

Types of Shuffling

There is no "tarot shuffle" out there, so I'm going to describe to you some of the most common ways to shuffle any kind of cards, and you can choose which one would work best for you.

OVERHAND SHUFFLE - this type of shuffling is the most common seen, where you gradually transfer the cards in the deck from back to front, middle to back. This is done by holding the deck in one hand, and using the opposite hand to transfer the cards.

RIFLE SHUFFLE - this is the shuffling type where you bend the cards, and flick them into each other using each thumb. This is the shuffle one would see at a poker table, sometimes with the cards coming back together in an arch. You definitely get a more complete shuffle using the Rifle method, but the cards do take a beating.

PILE SHUFFLE - instead of moving around individual cards, you split your deck into a number of small piles of say 5-10 cards, and then rearrange them back together. Doing this as many times as you'd like.

SMOOSHING - this is the shuffling we all did as kids, you lay your deck face down, and just smoosh them all over the table, catastrophically, and then putting them back together.

Cutting the Deck

After your done shuffling, whether you choose to always shuffle 5 times, or you're like me and you just shuffle until you feel like you're done shuffling, you cut your deck. And no, please don't go grab scissors.

Cutting the deck is when you split the deck into 3 (or 4, or 5, or 6...) piles and then put them back together in the order you see fit before pulling. This is again, not a necessary practice, and if you're using the pile method of shuffling, then you've kind of molded the two methods together anyway.

After I am done shuffling I split the deck into 3 piles and then rearrange. I think it's important to either stick with one way or to always switch it up, so that your deck understands what way you like best. (I switched up a method once and got the WEIRDEST reading ever.)

Pulling the Cards

If you're not ready to read reversed cards, you want to make sure you'll be flipping the cards off the deck so that they will come up facing the right way. This is usually a horizontal flip.

When you're ready to start reading reversed cards, you can either cut your deck, spin around a pile and shuffle in reversed cards, or just start changing how you flip the cards off the deck every once and a while. Maybe a few horizontal pulls and then a vertical flip.

START SMALL

Starting on your tarot journey can be really exciting, and it is very easy to want to jump into large and complicated spreads, especially if you're the type of person that likes to learn by doing. But even just staring with a card a day is still learning by doing, and it would do you well to start with a more simple and easy approach so you don't completely overload your brain.

Simply pulling a card a day can seem boring and tedious, but when you do pull your card in response to a question you've asked, take the time to really meditate on what you're looking at.

Are there symbols in the card that go along with the books interpretation that you may remember the next time you go to read that card. Is there anything on the card that stands out to you specifically at this time that maybe the guidebook doesn't reference and you feel you should look up? Like a crow or a daffodil that may seem like an insignificant background object, but nothing on a tarot cards illustration is insignificant or simple.

If you want to keep your learning incredibly simple, try and find a deck that isn't too heavy on the symbolism. My suggestions would be *The Wild Unknown Tarot* or *The Black Cats Tarot*, as their art is more "plain" and easier to read for beginners.

Other practices that fall into the "starting small" category are, don't read for others and working with reversed cards.

I know that when I first read for someone, I spent a lot of time looking up meanings in the guide book There's nothing wrong with that and I still do it from time to time now, but sometimes the interpretation in the book won't resonate with whoever you're reading for. There is a chance that if you were to go back later in your reading career and read the same cards for them again, it may make more sense as your intuition would have grown beyond the typed definition in the book. That being said, it is helpful to read for others to gain experience, but I would read for those you trust and who are open to the idea of tarot. If you are going to read for someone who is less than open to the occult or thinks it is hoaxy, you should be prepared for them to be negative and standoffish about it.

If you really want to try and open their eyes to divination, read the books description of the cards to them, and then use that information to put together your own interpretation depending on the spread that they have chosen. Trust your intuition when it comes to making your own interpretation. There will be thoughts or words or images that cross your mind when reading for others, and more often than not when I reveal this to the reader, they open up about how that pertains to their life in that moment.

Next is the reversed cards. Decks will always come printed the right way up and facing forward, so if you want to work with reversed cards you have to take the initiative to reverse them. This can be how you flip them off the deck, or turning cards around when you shuffle. If you chose not to work with reversed cards, the deck will find a suitable card that will help you to understand what they want to get across. Working with reversed cards though is not as hard as it may seem, or as hard as I thought it would be.

When a card is reversed, it is essentially giving you the opposite description of the right way up card. For some of the cards this can be pretty obvious. Reversed Strength = not feeling strong enough, feeling weak, not trusting your own strength, for instance.

If you really don't want to, you never have to work with reversed cards, but you will have to learn how to see the negative aspects to some of the "lighter" cards when they come up in spreads.

This of course only pertains to the decks that have reversed meanings.. Some artists don't give their decks reversed meanings and if a reversed card appears they will instruct you to simply flip it so it is the right way up.

Reading Bigger Spreads

When you start to read larger spreads, maybe 6, 7, 10 or 12 card spreads, there are some tips that I have found really helpful in getting used to putting them together.

No matter the size of the spread, the cards each have their individual meaning, and then they have a group meaning. It's like reading a paragraph one sentence at a time and deciphering it, then reading the whole paragraph and getting the bigger picture.

Take it slow when reading spreads with more cards, as it means more sentences and when the paragraph gets bigger it can take a while to fully understand. Connecting the first card to the tenth card may take some practice. Some of the larger spreads, like the wheel of the year, are good easy spreads to start with because each individual card is really just one card. Sometimes the card can connect to maybe the month or two before it or ahead of it, but usually this spread is one that gives you a general outlook on the next 12 months.

The Celtic Cross is a 10 card spread, where every card is connected to another one, and I always found I hard to look at this spread and think "yeah this makes sense."

If you never want to read anything over 5 or 6 cards, that's totally okay too!

What Affects a Reading?

Anything could affect how you read the cards, but since the deck is connected to you, the biggest factor will be you and where you are that day.

If you're exhausted, or grouchy, or have pumping adrenaline, or are distracted, this can affect how you read the cards and how they connect to you.

They are like kids in the way that they pick up on the energy of the holder and will respond accordingly. If you're worried about money but are trying to do a reading for love, there's a good chance you'll get more money advice in your spread which will just lead to confusion, especially if you're reading for someone else.

Before you do your reading, take some steps to make sure you are in the right frame of mind to do so, and this is where a pre-reading ritual comes in handy.

- do some grounding
- take a shower
- make a certain tea
- light incense
- get crystals
- get your tarot journal if you have one
- put on some music or turn everything off
- turn electronics off or to silent

Even after all of these, if you're still not really feeling like reading, or just feeling like something "isn't right", don't do the reading. You want to give yourself and your deck the utmost respect. If you're energy or mind frame just isn't there, don't force it, or else you could end up with a really wacky reading.

Asking Questions & Dealing With The Answers

When you or the person you're reading for, asks the deck a question, only ask it once. Don't ask the same question over and over, one spread after another, just because you don't like the answer.

I've never met a deck or a reader that will ask the deck the same question it was just asked, because well, that's pretty rude. You wouldn't keep asking someone the same question over and over if they gave you an answer you didn't like, and if you did they would probably just get frustrated with you and walk away. Decks and readers are the same way.

The answers you get from the deck, are the answers you need to hear at that time. The tarot doesn't owe you anything, doesn't owe you any kind of fluffy explanation or perfect answer. This is a tool that is supposed to help your introspection, not tell you what you want to hear.

If you treat your deck like this too often, chances are the deck will give up and just not tell you anything anymore. Why would they if you just question what they say?

DEALING WITH A NEGATIVE DECK

That being said, sometimes a deck is just done. Maybe there was a bad energy it picked up on and no matter what you do or how you cleanse it, it won't get rid of it. There really isn't a whole lot of rhyme or reason behind why a deck suddenly goes sour.

There are a few ways you'll know when your deck has "gone bad"

THE ANSWERS STOP MAKING SENSE - you've tried and tried and tried to understand what your deck is saying. You've sent photos of your cards to friends and even they can't interpret the meaning. It's like the cards are drunk and slurring their words.

EVERYTHING IS BAD - the deck has nothing good to say anymore. Everything is coming up The Devil or The Tower or the Three of Swords, all the time. No reading has any kid of positive undertone to it anymore, everything is just bad.

THE DECK DISAPPEARS - it's just, gone. You know where you put it, maybe it's in the same place you always put it, but it's not there. It's left the building, yeet.

IT FALLS APART - of course cards will fall apart with extensive use, but this is prematurely falling apart.

So what do you do when a deck starts to be sassy? You do what you can't do with people or naughty teenagers; you get rid of it.

We're not talking throwing it in the trash mind you, you still should be respectful, especially if it gave you a good chunk of time being your deck.

When I had to get rid of a negative deck, (the first deck that I already mentioned,) I burned it. One card at a time it went up in flames in my tiny little cauldron. It was the only way I could think to cleanse it of the negativity and set it free.

You don't have to do it as tediously as one card at a time if you have a fire pit or a wood burning stove, but I would say something nice, like "thank you for the last 5 years of service, I free you of your hold to me."

If you have a deck that isn't necessarily negative, but that you no longer connect with, you can always cleanse it and give it to someone else.

When I have "paid it forward" with tarot decks, I have a system;

~put the deck back in order
~cleanse the deck in some kind of incense smoke
~put it under the full moon light
~give it a selenite crystal

This is kind of like returning it to factory default settings before passing it on.

Creating Your Own Spreads

Why Create a Spread?

Sometimes, the questions you want to ask can't be confined to an already made spread. Or there's an energy about the day or the week or the year you want to be able to channel in a specific way. Creating your own spreads can be a wonderfully powerful way to connect and use your cards, as well as provide another reader with a different way of looking at things.

Where to Start

There are some things to consider when you go to make your own spread, and I break it down to who, what, where, when, why and how.

Who: who will this spread aimed at? Will it be a spread specific for you, or will it be aimed at a situation?

What: what are you hoping to gain from this spread? Clarity on a situation? The outcome of a decision? Emotional understanding?

WHERE: is what you're asking for happening somewhere specific? Does it affect your mind? Your body? Your soul? Your family? Your home?

WHEN: is the spread specific to a time frame? Early future? Distant past? Something happening in the present?

WHY: why are you requesting the clarification or help? Are you stuck? Are you worried? Are you anxious? Are you confused?

HOW: the how is like your outcome. How will I take hold of the future? How long will it take? How do I fix my mistake? How do I open up?

These are all things to consider when you're making up your own spreads, even if you're being inspired by an event or an astrological alignment. Everything has a certain energy, and when you create a spread you're essentially organizing that energy in a way that is most beneficial to you and helps you understand it.

Choosing the Shape

The spread shape can have as much significance or not as you desire. If you're creating a spread to channel the energy of a zodiac sign, maybe you want the shape to mimic the sign of the zodiac. This *can* end up being a lot of cards, so I suggest making up your questions before you make up your shape.

If you want to keep it simple with 3 or 4 cards, there really is only so many shapes you can make with that amount. Horizontal or vertical lines, triangles, or squares. If you create a spread using 5 or more cards, you'll have more opportunity for different shapes or designs.

I have tried creating the spread shape to what I wanted them to look like, but then coming up with all the right questions for the cards proved too difficult and I ended up changing it anyway.

Try not to overthink the shape of it too much, or that it is too similar to someone else's spread. As long as you're not copying that persons questions and trying to pass it off as your own, your spread will be fine.

SINGLE CARD PULLS

This list of single card pulls is of course only a suggestion, there will be days or evenings where these cards won't make sense for you, and that's okay! These are here as a starting point for pulling a card every day or every evening in order to get practice in reading.

MORNING

- WHAT SHOULD I LOOK OUT FOR TODAY
- WHAT IS SOMETHING TO REMEMBER TODAY
- WHAT WILL TODAY BRING ME
- WHAT ENERGY SHOULD I CHANNEL
- WHAT ASPECT SHOULD I WORK ON
- HOW WOULD YOU GUIDE ME TODAY
- WHAT IS TODAY'S THEME
- HOW CAN I BE BETTER/IMPROVE TODAY
- WHAT'S MY BIGGEST CHALLENGE TODAY
- WHERE AM I BEING CALLED TO, TO SHARE MY STRENGTHS TODAY
- WHAT DO I NEED TO FOCUS MY ATTENTION TO TODAY
- WHAT DO YOU HAVE TO TELL ME
- WHAT MIGHT BLOCK ME TODAY

EVENING

- WHAT WAS TODAYS LESSON
- WHERE COULD I HAVE BEEN BETTER TODAY
- HOW COULD I HAVE OVERCOME OBSTACLES TODAY
- WHAT WAS MY DOWNFALL TODAY
- WHAT DID I TEACH OTHERS TODAY
- WHERE WAS I INSPIRED TODAY
- WHERE DID I INSPIRE TODAY
- WHAT WAS MY WEAKEST POINT TODAY
- WHAT WAS MY STRONGEST POINT TODAY
- WHAT CAN I TAKE FROM TODAY TO HELP ME TOMORROW

2 Card Pulls

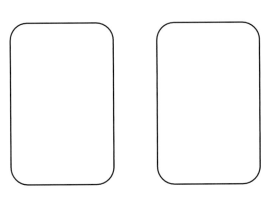

THE BLOCKAGE	THE REMOVER
THE PROBLEM	THE SOLUTION
THE ILLUSION	THE REALITY
CONTRIBUTING FACTOR	OPPOSING FACTOR
LIGHT SELF	SHADOW SELF
GROWING ASPECT	SHEDDING ASPECT
FEMININE SIDE	MASCULINE SIDE
MY JOY	MY SADNESS
MY FEAR	MY COURAGE
NATURE	NUTURE
PRODUCTIVITY	DISTRACTION
INNER FIGHTER	OUTER FIGHTER

3 Card Pulls

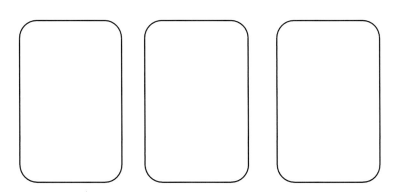

Past	Present	Future
Body	Mind	Soul
Subconscious	Conscious	Superconscious
Child	Parent	Adult
Illusion	Knowledge	Magic
The Star	Opposition	Outcome
Idea	Plan	Carry Out
Face	Embrace	Erase
External Influence	Internal Influence	Outward Decision

JANUARY

Sun	Mon	Tue	Wed
3	4	5	6
10	11	12	13
17	18	19	20
24	25	26	27
31			

Thu	Fri	Sat	
	1	2	**New Moon** Capricorn 23° Stellium in Capricorn— Sun, Moon & Pluto (Saturn conjunct Jupiter,) Square Mars Venus Trine Uranus
7	8	9	**Full Moon** Leo 9° Sun conj. Jupiter Sun/Saturn square Uranus Square Moon Pluto conj. Venus
14	15	16	
21	22	23	
28	29	30	

Last Qtr Moon	Jan 6, Libra
New Moon	Jan 13, Aqua
First Qtr Moon	Jan 20, Taurus
Full Moon	Jan 28, Leo

The Month Ahead

- PERSONAL CHALLENGE
- PERSONAL GROWTH
- YOU AT THE MONTHS START
- YOU AT THE MONTHS END
- EXTERNAL OBSTACLE
- JANUARY THEME/ENERGY

YOU AT THE MONTHS START: _____

_____

_____

PERSONAL CHALLENGE _____

_____

_____

EXTERNAL OBSTACLE: _____

_____

_____

Personal growth: _____

_____

_____

January's theme/energy _____

_____

_____

You at the months end:_____

_____

_____

Take a moment to write down or draw, any feelings, visions or thoughts that have arisen from the cards you pulled for this month.

JANUARY

Week In Advance

1 _____

Monday 4

Tuesday 5

Wednesday 6

2 _____

3 _____

Thursday 7

Friday 8

Saturday 9

Sunday 10

JANUARY
New Moon in Capricorn

I KNOW I AM STRONG, FORMIDABLE & UNWAVERING. I DON'T MOVE MOUNTAINS, I BECOME ONE. EVERLASTING & ABLE TO BRAVE ANY STORM. THERE IS NOTHING I CAN'T DO.

1. WHERE DO I FEEL MOST STABLE
2. WHAT THREATENS MY STABILITY
3. WHAT DO I DO WHEN I FEEL UNSTABLE
4. HOW DO I REACT WHEN MY STABILITY IS THREATENED
5. HOW TO STRENGTHEN MY FOUNDATION
6. MY STRENGTH REMINDER

1. WHERE DO I FEEL MOST STABLE _____
_____
_____
_____
_____

2. WHAT THREATENS MY STABILITY _____
_____
_____
_____
_____

3. WHAT DO I DO WHEN I FEEL UNSTABLE _____
_____
_____
_____
_____

4. HOW DO I REACT WHEN MY STABILITY IS THREATENED _____
_____
_____
_____
_____

5. HOW TO STRENGTHEN MY FOUNDATION _____
_____
_____
_____
_____

6. MY STRENGTH REMINDER _____
_____
_____
_____

JANUARY

Week In Advance

Monday — 11

Tuesday — 12

Wednesday — 13 ●

Thursday 14

_____
_____
_____
_____
_____
_____

Friday 15

_____
_____
_____
_____
_____
_____

Saturday 16

_____
_____
_____
_____
_____
_____

Sunday 17

_____
_____
_____
_____
_____
_____

JANUARY

Week In Advance

Monday — 18

Tuesday — 19

Wednesday — 20

Thursday 21

Friday 22

Saturday 23

Sunday 24

JANUARY

Week In Advance

Monday — 25

Tuesday — 26

Wednesday — 27

Thursday 28

Friday 29

Saturday 30

Sunday 31

JANUARY
Full Wolf Moon in Leo

By going after my passions, I can sustain the fire in my heart, I release those that hold me back, and move forward to stand in my own light

1. What is the tie preventing me from progressing forward
2. How can I burn the tie
3. What can the Leo fire ignite in me
4. What door is closing
5. What door is opening

1. WHAT IS THE TIE PREVENTING ME FROM PROGRESSING FORWARD

_____

_____

_____

2. HOW CAN I BURN THE TIE _____

_____

_____

_____

3. WHAT CAN THE LEO FIRE IGNITE IN ME _____

_____

_____

_____

4. WHAT DOOR IS CLOSING _____

_____

_____

_____

5. WHAT DOOR IS OPENING _____

_____

_____

_____

FEBRUARY

Sun	Mon	Tue	Wed
	1	2	3
7	8	9	10
14	15	16	17
21	22	23	24
28			

Thu	Fri	Sat	
4	5	6	**New Moon** Aquarius 23° Sun, Moon Mercury, Venus & Jupiter in Aquarius
11	12	13	Venus conj. Jupiter Mars square all Aqua. Planets Mars trine Neptune
18	19	20	**Full Moon** Virgo 8° Sun sextile Uranus Moon trine Uranus Venus exalted Mars trine Pluto Mars sextile Neptune
25	26	27	

FEBRUARY

- ◐ Last Qtr Moon — Feb 4, Libra
- ● New Moon — Feb 11, Aqua
- ◑ First Qtr Moon — Feb 19, Taurus
- ○ Full Moon — Feb 27, Leo

The Month Ahead

- YOU AT THE MONTHS START
- PERSONAL CHALLENGE
- PERSONAL GROWTH
- YOU AT THE MONTHS END
- EXTERNAL OBSTACLE
- FEBRUARY THEME/ENERGY

YOU AT THE MONTHS START: _____

_____

_____

PERSONAL CHALLENGE _____

_____

_____

EXTERNAL OBSTACLE: _____

_____

Personal growth: _____
_____
_____

February's theme/energy _____
_____
_____

You at the months end:_____
_____
_____

Take a moment to write down or draw, any feelings, visions or thoughts that have arisen from the cards you pulled for this month.

FEBRUARY

Week In Advance

Monday 1

Tuesday 2

Wednesday 3

Thursday 4

Friday 5

Saturday 6

Sunday 7

FEBRUARY

Week In Advance

Monday 8

Tuesday 9

Wednesday 10

Thursday 11

Friday 12

Saturday 13

Sunday 14

FEBRUARY
New Moon in Aquarius

1. WHY DO I SHY AWAY FROM MY TRUE SELF
2. WHAT DO I LOVE MOST ABOUT ME
3. HOW CAN I SHOW THE WORLD WHO I AM
4. WHERE DOES MY PURPOSE LIE

I HAVE A PLACE IN THIS WORLD ~ ONE THAT ALLOWS ME TO BE UNIQUELY WHO I AM. I NEED NOT COMPARE MYSELF TO OTHERS, BUT INSTEAD OWN MYSELF WHOLLY. I AM IMPORTANT & I HAVE PURPOSE

1. WHY DO I SHAY AWAY FROM MY TRUE SELF_____
_____
_____
_____
_____

2. WHAT DO I LOVE MOST ABOUT ME_____
_____
_____
_____
_____

3. HOW CAN I SHOW THE WORLD WHO I AM_____
_____
_____
_____
_____

4. WHERE DOES MY PURPOSE LIE_____
_____
_____
_____
_____

FEBRUARY

Week In Advance

Monday　15

Tuesday　16

Wednesday　17

Thursday 18

Friday 19

Saturday 20

Sunday 21

FEBRUARY

Week In Advance

Monday   22

Tuesday   23

Wednesday   24

Thursday 25

Friday 26

Saturday 27

Sunday 28

FEBRUARY
Full Ice Moon in Virgo

MY VESSEL IS IMPORTANT. I RESPECT & HONOUR MY BOUNDARIES & LET GO OF OLD HABITS THAT NO LONGER SERVE ME. I FIND PEACE IN MY OWN BEING

1. HOW I CURRENTLY SEE THE STATE OF MY BODY
2. HOW I CURRENTLY SEE THE STATE OF MY MIND
3. HOW I CURRENTLY SEE THE STATE OF MY SOUL
4. WHAT IS NO LONGER SERVING MY BODY
5. WHAT IS NO LONGER SERVING MY MIND
6. WHAT IS NO LONGER SERVING MY SOUL
7. WHAT IS A BOUNDARY PROTECTING MY BODY
8. WHAT IS A BOUNDARY PROTECTING MY MIND
9. WHAT IS A BOUNDARY PROTECTING MY SOUL

How I currently see the state of me;
Body _____
_____

Mind _____
_____

Soul _____
_____

What is no longer serving my;
Body _____
_____

Mind _____
_____

Soul _____
_____

What is a boundary protecting my;
Body _____
_____

Mind _____
_____

Soul _____
_____

MARCH

SUN	MON	TUE	WED
	1	2	3
7	8	9	10
14	15	16	17
21	22	23	24
28	29	30	31

Thu	Fri	Sat
4	5	6
11	12	13
18	19	20
25	26	27

New Moon
PISCES 23°
SUN & MOON
CONJ. NEPTUNE
& VENUS
PISCES STELLIUM
SEXTILE PLUTO
SATURN SQUARE
URANUS
MARS TRINE
SATURN

Full Moon
LIBRA 8°
SUN CONJ.
VENUS &
CHIRON
GRAND AIR
TRINE: SATURN,
MARS & MOON
MERCURY CONJ.
NEPTUNE
SUN SEXTILE
SATURN

Last Qtr Moon	Mar 5, Libra
New Moon	Mar 15, Aqua
First Qtr Moon	Mar 21, Taurus
Full Moon	Mar 28, Leo

The Month Ahead

- PERSONAL CHALLENGE
- PERSONAL GROWTH
- YOU AT THE MONTHS START
- YOU AT THE MONTHS END
- EXTERNAL OBSTACLE
- MARCH THEME/ENERGY

YOU AT THE MONTHS START: _____
_____
_____

PERSONAL CHALLENGE _____
_____
_____

EXTERNAL OBSTACLE: _____
_____
_____

Personal growth: _____
_____
_____

March's theme/energy _____
_____
_____

You at the months end:_____
_____
_____

Take a moment to write down or draw, any feelings, visions or thoughts
that have arisen from the cards you pulled for this month.

MARCH

Week In Advance

Monday 1

Tuesday 2

Wednesday 3

Thursday 4

Friday 5

Saturday 6

Sunday 7

MARCH

Week In Advance

Monday — 8

Tuesday — 9

Wednesday — 10

Thursday 11

Friday 12

Saturday 13

Sunday 14

MARCH
New Moon in Pisces

1. What lies dormant in my soul
2. How am I being supported
3. What is it I think I want
4. What do I actually need
5. Where is my inspiration coming from

I AM SUPPORTED BY THE UNIVERSE. ANYTHING I WISH TO CREATE CAN BE MIND, SO LONG AS IT COMES FROM THE SOUL. I AM INSPIRED & READY TO LIVE MY LIFE AS I HAVE ALWAYS DREAMED.

1. WHAT LIES DORMANT IN MY SOUL _____
_____
_____
_____

2. HOW AM I BEING SUPPORTED _____
_____
_____
_____

3. WHAT IS IT I THINK I WANT _____
_____
_____
_____

4. WHAT DO I ACTUALLY NEED _____
_____
_____
_____

5. WHERE IS MY INSPIRTATION COMING FROM _____
_____
_____
_____

MARCH

Week In Advance

Monday 15

Tuesday 16

Wednesday 17

Thursday 18

Friday 19

Saturday 20

Sunday 21

MARCH

Week In Advance

Monday 22

Tuesday 23

Wednesday 24

Thursday 25

Friday 26

Saturday 27

Sunday 28

MARCH
Full Storm Moon in Libra

1. WHAT PART OF MY PAST HAS ALREADY HEALED
2. WHAT PART AM I CURRENTLY HEALING
3. HOW WILL THIS RESTORE MY BALANCE
4. WHAT WILL THIS LIGHT UP IN ME

I AM HEALING FROM MY PAST TO CREATE BALANCE IN MY LIFE. I HAVE COMPASSION FOR MYSELF & OTHERS THROUGH THE PROCESS. SOON, I WILL BE ENTERING A NEW PHASE OF LIFE

1. WHAT PART OF MY PAST HAS ALREADY HEALED _____
_____
_____
_____

2. WHAT PART AM I CURRENTLY HEALING _____
_____
_____
_____

3. HOW WILL THIS RESTORE MY BALANCE _____
_____
_____
_____

4. WHAT WILL THIS LIGHT UP IN ME _____
_____
_____
_____

APRIL

SUN	MON	TUE	WED
4	5	6	7
11	12	13	14
18	19	20	21
25	26	27	28

Thu	Fri	Sat
1	2	3
8	9	10
15	16	17
22	23	24
29	30	

New Moon
ARIES 22°
SUN & MOON CONJ. VENUS & SEXTILE JUPITER
SUN & MOON SQUARE PLUTO
SUN & MOON SEXTILE MARS
MERCURY SEXTILE SATURN

Full Moon
SCORPIO 7°
SUN & MOON SQUARE SATURN
SUN CONJ. URANUS
URANUS CONJ. VENUS
MERCURY CONJ. VENUS & LILLITH
SUN & MOON SEXTILE MARS

Last Qtr Moon — Apr 4, Libra
New Moon — Apr 11, Aqua
First Qtr Moon — Ape. 20 Taurus
Full Moon — Apr 26, Leo

The Month Ahead

- Personal Challenge
- Personal Growth
- You at the months start
- You at the months end
- External Obstacle
- April Theme/Energy

You at the months start: _____

_____

_____

Personal challenge _____

_____

_____

External obstacle: _____

_____

_____

Personal growth: _____

_____

_____

April's theme/energy _____

_____

_____

You at the months end:_____

_____

_____

Take a moment to write down or draw, any feelings, visions or thoughts that have arisen from the cards you pulled for this month.

APRIL

Week In Advance

Monday — 29

Tuesday — 30

Wednesday — 31

Thursday 1

Friday 2

Saturday 3

Sunday 4

Week In Advance

Monday 5

Tuesday 6

Wednesday 7

Thursday 8

Friday 9

Saturday 10

Sunday 11

APRIL
New Moon in Aries

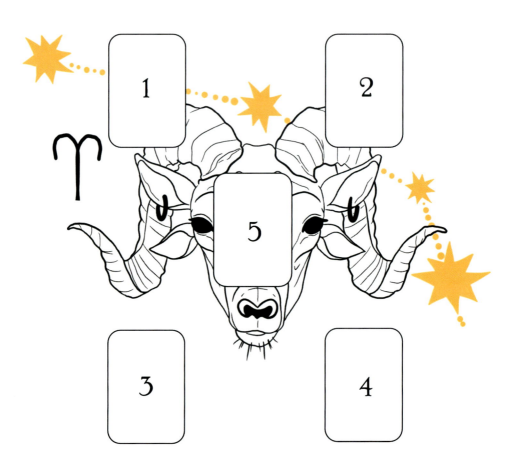

1. WHAT ARE THE ASHES BENEATH ME MADE FROM
2. I AM RISING WITH WHAT STRENGTH
3. WHERE WILL I TAKE MY SOUL FROM HERE
4. THIS IS THE ENERGY I SHOULD TAP INTO
5. THIS FOCAL POINT WILL HELP SHAPE MY WORLD

I AM RENEWED, REFRESHED & REBORN. I HAVE THE WORLD IN MY HANDS, & I AM THE CREATOR OF MY OWN DESTINY. I AM PURE ENERGY IN MOTION.

1. WHAT ARE THE ASHES BENEATH ME MADE OF _____
_____
_____
_____
_____

2. I AM RISING WITH WHAT STRENGTH _____
_____
_____
_____
_____

3. WHERE WILL I TAKE MY SOUL FROM HERE _____
_____
_____
_____
_____

4. THIS IS THE ENERGY I SHOULD TAP INTO _____
_____
_____
_____
_____

5. THIS FOCAL POINT WILL HELP SHAPE MY WORLD _____
_____
_____
_____

APRIL

Week In Advance

Monday — 12

___

Tuesday — 13

___

Wednesday — 14

___

Thursday 15

Friday 16

Saturday 17

Sunday 18

APRIL

Week In Advance

Monday — 19

_____
_____
_____
_____
_____
_____

Tuesday — 20 ◐

_____
_____
_____
_____
_____
_____

Wednesday — 21

_____
_____
_____
_____
_____

Thursday 22

Friday 23

Saturday 24

Sunday 25

APRIL

Week In Advance

Monday — 26

Tuesday — 27

Wednesday — 28

Thursday 29

Friday 30

Saturday 1

Sunday 2

APRIL
Full Growing Moon in Scorpio

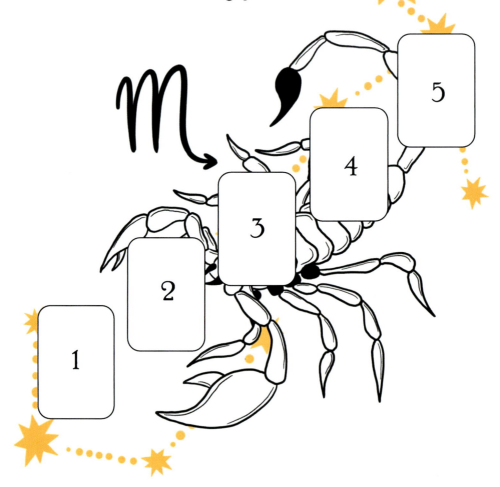

1. My wings are supported by this
2. What is my personal truth
3. What have I left behind
4. What is my personal strength
5. The light ahead illuminates this

I HAVE UNEARTHED THE TRUTH. THERE IS NO GOING BACK NOW. I HAVE FALLEN A THROUSAND TIMES, BUT NOW I WILL FIND THE WILL TO RISE.
A PHOENIX BURNING

1. WHAT LIES DORMANT IN MY SOUL _____
_____
_____
_____
_____

2. HOW AM I BEING SUPPORTED _____
_____
_____
_____
_____

3. WHAT IS IT I THINK I WANT _____
_____
_____
_____
_____

4. WHAT DO I ACTUALLY NEED _____
_____
_____
_____
_____

5. WHERE IS MY INSPIRTATION COMING FROM _____
_____
_____
_____

MAY

Sun	Mon	Tue	Wed
2	3	4	5
9	10	11	12
16	17	18	19
23	24	25	26
30	31		

○ Lunar Eclipse

Thu	Fri	Sat	
		1	**New Moon** Taurus 21° Sun & Moon conj. Lillith Mars sextile Uranus Mercury conj. North Node
6	7	8	Sun & Moon sextile Neptune Mercury sextile Saturn
13	14	15	**Full Moon** Sag 5° - Eclipse Sun conj. North Node Mercury conj. Venus North Node sextile Chiron Sun & Moon square Jupiter Mercury in Domicile
20	21	22	
27	28	29	

Last Qtr Moon — May 3, Libra
New Moon — May 11 Aqua
First Qtr Moon — May 19 Taurus
Full Moon — May 26, Leo

The Month Ahead

- PERSONAL CHALLENGE
- PERSONAL GROWTH
- YOU AT THE MONTHS START
- YOU AT THE MONTHS END
- EXTERNAL OBSTACLE
- MAY THEME/ENERGY

YOU AT THE MONTHS START: _____

_____

_____

PERSONAL CHALLENGE _____

_____

_____

EXTERNAL OBSTACLE: _____

_____

_____

Personal growth: _____
_____
_____

May's theme/energy _____
_____
_____

You at the months end:_____
_____
_____

Take a moment to write down or draw, any feelings, visions or thoughts that have arisen from the cards you pulled for this month.

MAY

Week In Advance

Monday — 3

Tuesday — 4

Wednesday — 5

Thursday 6

Friday 7

Saturday 8

Sunday 9

MAY

Week In Advance

Monday — 10

Tuesday — 11 ●

Wednesday — 12

Thursday 13

_____
_____
_____
_____
_____

Friday 14

_____
_____
_____
_____
_____

Saturday 15

_____
_____
_____
_____

Sunday 16

_____
_____
_____
_____

MAY
New Moon in Taurus

I EMBRACE MY MAGIC & STAND IN MY RAW POWER. I MANIFEST MY FUTURE BY SPEAKING MY DESTINY INTO EXISTENCE. I KNOW THE VALUE OF MY INTENTIONS.

1. THE EARTH PROVIDES ME WITH THIS STABILITY
2. THE AIR PROVIDES ME WITH THIS KNOWLEDGE
3. THE WATER PROVIDES ME WITH THIS ADAPTABILITY
4. THE FIRE PROVIDES ME WITH THIS STRENGTH
5. MY POWER AWAKENS THIS IN ME
6. I WILL STRENGTHEN MY POWER WITH THIS

1. The Earth provides me with this stability _____
_____
_____
_____

2. The Air provides me with this knowledge _____
_____
_____
_____

3. The Water provides me with this adaptability _____
_____
_____
_____

4. The Fire provides me with this strength _____
_____
_____
_____

5. My power awakens this in me _____
_____
_____
_____

6. I will strengthen my power with this _____
_____
_____
_____

MAY

Week In Advance

Monday — 17

Tuesday — 18

Wednesday — 19

Thursday 20

Friday 21

Saturday 22

Sunday 23

MAY

Week In Advance

Monday — 24

Tuesday — 25

Wednesday — 26
Lunar Eclipse

Thursday 27

Friday 28

Saturday 29

Sunday 30

MAY
Full Hare Moon in Sagittarius

Not everything is in my control, but I choose to go with the changes. I find a place between my past & future. I am present. I am here. I am healing.

1. How I manage not being in control
2. What changes are the hardest for me
3. What changes are the easiest for me
4. How will letting go help me heal
5. What I need to remember about the past
6. What I look forward to in the future

1. HOW I MANAGE BEING IN CONTROL _____
_____
_____
_____

2. WHAT CHANGES ARE THE HARDEST FOR ME _____
_____
_____
_____

3. WHAT CHANGES ARE THE EASIEST FOR ME _____
_____
_____
_____

4. HOW WILL LETTING GO HELP ME HEAL _____
_____
_____
_____

5. WHAT I NEED TO REMEMBER ABOUT THE PAST _____
_____
_____
_____

6. WHAT I LOOK FORWARD TO IN THE FUTURE _____
_____
_____
_____

JUNE

Sun	Mon	Tue	Wed
		1	2
6	7	8	9
13	14	15	16
20	21	22	23
27	28	29	30

Thu	Fri	Sat
3	4	5
10	11	12
● Solar Eclipse		
17	18	19
◐		
24	25	26
○		

New Moon
Gemini 19°
- Eclipse
Sun & Moon
conj. Mercury
Mars opposite
Pluto
Venus sectile
Uranus

Full Moon
Capricorn 3°
Sun trine
Jupiter
Moon sextile
Jupiter
Venus opposite
Pluto
Venus trine
Neptune
Mercury trine
Saturn
Mars opposite
Saturn

Last Qtr Moon — June 2, Libra
New Moon — June 10, Aqua
First Qtr Moon — June 17 Taurus
Full Moon — June 24 Leo

The Month Ahead

- Personal Challenge
- Personal Growth
- You at the Months Start
- You at the Months End
- External Obstacle
- June Theme/Energy

You at the months start: _____

_____

_____

Personal challenge _____

_____

_____

External obstacle: _____

_____

_____

Personal growth: _____
_____
_____

June's theme/energy _____
_____
_____

You at the months end:_____
_____
_____

Take a moment to write down or draw, any feelings, visions or thoughts that have arisen from the cards you pulled for this month.

JUNE

Week In Advance

Monday — 31

Tuesday — 1

Wednesday — 2

Thursday 3

Friday 4

Saturday 5

Sunday 6

JUNE

Week In Advance

Monday   7

Tuesday   8

Wednesday   9

Thursday
Solar Eclipse

10

Friday

11

Saturday

12

Sunday

13

JUNE
New Moon in Gemini

1. How can I make sure to express myself with authenticity
2. How far does my energy reach
3. What do I lose from speaking these truths
4. How to accept not everyone will accept it

I SPEAK FROM THE HEART. I EXPRESS MYSELF WHOLLY & UNAPOLOGETICALLY. EVERY WORD COMES POURING OUT OF ME, FILLING THE SPACE WITH MY ENERGY.
IT IS PURE ALCHEMY

1. HOW CAN I MAKE SURE TO EXPRESS MYSELF WITH AUTHENTICITY_____
_____
_____
_____

2. HOW FAR DOES MY ENERGY REACH_____
_____
_____
_____

3. WHAT DO I LOSE FROM SPEAKING THESE TRUTHS_____
_____
_____
_____

4. HOW TO ACCEPT NOT EVERYONE WILL ACCEPT IT_____
_____
_____
_____

JUNE

Week In Advance

Monday 14

Tuesday 15

Wednesday 16

Thursday 17

Friday 18

Saturday 19

Sunday 20

JUNE

Week In Advance

Monday 21

Tuesday 22

Wednesday 23

Thursday 24

Friday 25

Saturday 26

Sunday 27

JUNE
Full Mead Moon in Capricorn

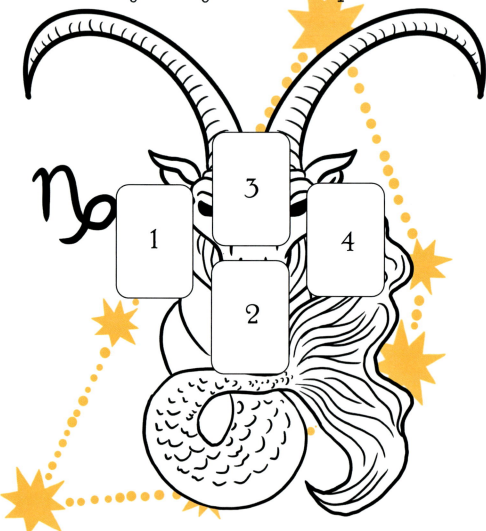

1. Where do I begin building
2. What is my first step when working towards my dreams
3. How do I keep my manifestations growing
4. What do my goals require of me daily

THE STRUCTURES I BUILD ARE LASTING & BOUNTIFUL.
THEY CREATE SPACE FOR MY DREAMS TO THRIVE.
I CAN MANIFEST THEM INTO REALITY,

1. WHERE DO I BEGIN BUILDING _____
_____
_____
_____

2. WHAT IS MY FIRST STEP WHEN WORKING TOWARDS MY DREAMS
_____
_____
_____

3. HOW DO I KEEP MY MANIFESTATIONS GROWING _____
_____
_____
_____

4. WHAT DO MY GOALS REQUIRE OF ME DAILY _____
_____
_____
_____

JULY

Sun	Mon	Tue	Wed
4	5	6	7
11	12	13	14
18	19	20	21
25	26	27	28

Thu	Fri	Sat
1	2	3
8	9	10
15	16	17
22	23	24
29	30	31

New Moon
Cancer 18°
Sun & Moon sextile Uranus
Mercury square Neptune
Venus conj. Mars
Venus opposite Saturn

Full Moon
Aquarius 1°
Mercury trine Neptune
Mercury opposite Pluto
Venus opposite Jupiter
Mars opposite Jupiter

JULY

◐ Last Qtr Moon — July 1, Libra
● New Moon — July 9, Aqua
◑ First Qtr Moon — July 17 Taurus
○ Full Moon — July 23 Leo
◐ Last Qtr Moon — July 31

The Month Ahead

- Personal Challenge
- Personal Growth
- You at the Months Start
- You at the Months End
- External Obstacle
- July Theme/Energy

You at the months start: _____

_____

_____

Personal challenge _____

_____

_____

External obstacle: _____

_____

_____

Personal growth: _____

_____

_____

July's theme/energy _____

_____

_____

You at the months end:_____

_____

_____

Take a moment to write down or draw, any feelings, visions or thoughts that have arisen from the cards you pulled for this month.

JULY

Week In Advance

Monday — 28

Tuesday — 29

Wednesday — 30

Thursday 1

Friday 2

Saturday 3

Sunday 4

JULY

Week In Advance

Monday — 5

Tuesday — 6

Wednesday — 7

Thursday 8

Friday 9

Saturday 10

Sunday 11

JULY

New Moon in Cancer

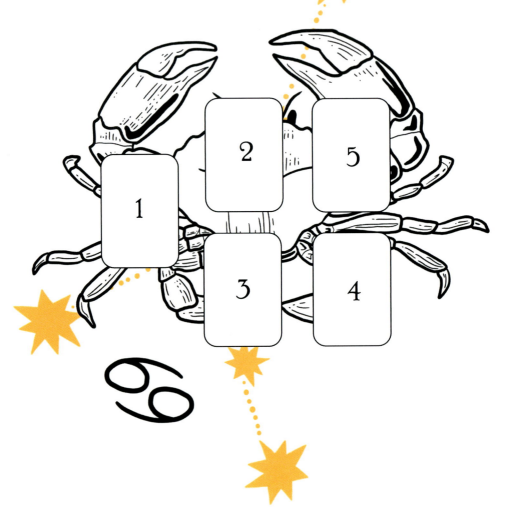

1. How do I feel when alone
2. What is healed between my inner self & my past
3. How does my peace effect my every day
4. My soul requires this
5. My home requires this

I FIND SOLACE N MY WINNER WORLD & HONOUR MY PAST. THERE IS PEACE WITHIN ME. I NOURISH MY SOUL. I AM HOME NOW.

1. How do I feel when alone_____
_____
_____
_____

2. What is healed between my inner self & my past_____
_____
_____
_____

3. How does my peace effect my every day_____
_____
_____
_____

4. My soul requires this_____
_____
_____
_____

5. My home requires this_____
_____
_____
_____

JULY

Week In Advance

Monday — 12

Tuesday — 13

Wednesday — 14

Thursday 15

Friday 16

Saturday 17

Sunday 18

JULY

Week In Advance

Monday 19

Tuesday 20

Wednesday 21

Thursday 22

___

Friday 23

___

Saturday 24

Sunday 25

JULY
Full Hay Moon in Aquarius

1. What wall must I break through
2. How do I find the tools to build
3. What has been holding me back
4. Where do the boundaries of my comfort zone lie
5. How will I feel when I break these boundaries

To grow is to get uncomfortable. I can't wait for a future that I long for. I must create it. The future is now.

1. What wall must I break through _____
_____
_____
_____

2. How do if ind the tools to build _____
_____
_____
_____

3. What has been holding me back _____
_____
_____
_____

4. Where do the boundaries of my comfort zone lie _____
_____
_____
_____

5. How will I feel when I break these boundaries _____
_____
_____
_____

JULY

Week In Advance

Monday — 26

Tuesday — 27

Wednesday — 28

Thursday 29

Friday 30

Saturday 31

Sunday 1

AUGUST

Sun	Mon	Tue	Wed
1	2	3	4
8	9	10	11
15	16	17	18
22	23	24	25
29	30	31	

Thu	Fri	Sat
5	6	7
12	13	14
19	20	21
26	27	28

New Moon
Leo 16°
Sun & Moon square Uranus
Mercury opposite Jupiter
Venus opposite Jupiter
Venus trine Pluto

Full Moon
Aquarius 29°
Sun opposite Jupiter
Moon conj. Jupiter
Mars trine Uranus
Mercury opposite Neptune
Venus trine Saturn

Last Qtr Moon — Aug 30 Libra
New Moon — Aug 8 Aqua
First Qtr Moon — Aug 15 Taurus
Full Moon — Aug 22 Leo

The Month Ahead

- Personal Challenge
- Personal Growth
- You at the Months Start
- You at the Months End
- External Obstacle
- August Theme/Energy

You at the months start: _____
_____
_____

Personal challenge _____
_____
_____

External obstacle: _____
_____
_____

Personal growth: _____
_____
_____

August's theme/energy _____
_____
_____

You at the months end: _____
_____
_____

Take a moment to write down or draw, any feelings, visions or thoughts that have arisen from the cards you pulled for this month.

AUGUST

Week In Advance

Monday — 2

Tuesday — 3

Wednesday — 4

Thursday 5

Friday 6

Saturday 7

Sunday 8

AUGUST
New Moon in Leo

1. What is a feeling I have long forgotten
2. How can I nourish my inner child
3. My inner child is dormant, what will wake them
4. What is a daily pleasure I can find again
5. What about me do I love the most

I FIND JOY IN MY OWN BEING. I CREATE THE HAPPINESS I DESERVE. STARTING TODAY, I MAKE SPACE FOR MY |INNER~CHILD & WELCOME PLEASURE BACK INTO MY LIFE.

1. WHAT IS A FEELING I HAVE LONG FORGOTTEN _____
_____
_____
_____
_____

2. HOW CAN I NOURISH MY INNER CHILD _____
_____
_____
_____
_____

3. MY INNER CHILD IS DORMANT, WHAT WILL WAKE THEM _____
_____
_____
_____
_____

4. WHAT IS A DAILY PLEASURE I CAN FIND AGAIN _____
_____
_____
_____
_____

5. WHERE ABOUT ME DO I LOVE THE MOST _____
_____
_____
_____
_____

AUGUST

Week In Advance

Monday — 9

Tuesday — 10

Wednesday — 11

Thursday 12

Friday 13

Saturday 14

Sunday 15

AUGUST

Week In Advance

Monday — 16

Tuesday — 17

Wednesday — 18

Thursday 19

Friday 20

Saturday 21

Sunday 22

AUGUST
Full Corn Moon in Aquarius

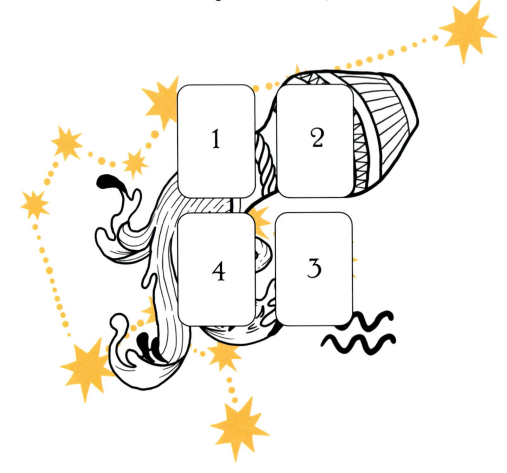

1. PAST ME WOULD TELL ME THIS
2. PRESENT ME GIVES ME STRENGTH VIA THIS
3. AS I LET THE PAST GO, I FEEL THIS
4. THE FUTURE I CREATE WILL BRING OUT THIS IN ME

I AM TRANSITIONING. I RELEASE MY PAST & WELCOME WHAT IS TO COME. THERE IS HOPE IN THE FUTURE. I AM READY TO EMBRACE IT.

1. PAST ME WOULD TELL ME THIS _____
_____
_____
_____

2. PRESENT ME GIVES ME STRENGTH VIA THIS _____
_____
_____
_____

3. AS I LET THE PAST GO, I FEEL THIS _____
_____
_____
_____

4. THE FUTURE I CREATE WILL BRING OUT THIS IN ME _____
_____
_____
_____

AUGUST

Week In Advance

Monday 22

Tuesday 23

Wednesday 24

Thursday 25

Friday 26

Saturday 27

Sunday 28

SEPTEMBER

Sun	Mon	Tue	Wed
			1
5	6 ●	7	8
12	13 ◐	14	15
19	20 ○	21	22
26	27	28	29

Thu	Fri	Sat
2	3	4
9	10	11
16	17	18
23	24	25
30		

New Moon
Virgo 14°
Sun & Moon trine Uranus
Mars trine Pluto
Mercury trine Saturn
Mars opposite Neptune
Venus trine Jupiter
Venus square Pluto

Full Moon
Pisces 28°
Sun conj. Mars
Sun trine Pluto
Moon sextile Pluto
Mercury trine Jupiter
Venus opposite Uranus
Venus square Saturn
Mars trine Saturn

SEPTEMBER

Last Qtr Moon — Sept 28 Libra
New Moon — Sept 6 Aqua
First Qtr Moon — Sept 13 Taurus
Full Moon — Sept 20 Leo

The Month Ahead

- PERSONAL CHALLENGE
- PERSONAL GROWTH
- YOU AT THE MONTHS START
- YOU AT THE MONTHS END
- EXTERNAL OBSTACLE
- SEPTEMBER THEME/ ENERGY

YOU AT THE MONTHS START: _____
_____
_____

PERSONAL CHALLENGE _____
_____
_____

EXTERNAL OBSTACLE: _____
_____
_____

Personal growth: _____

_____

_____

September's theme/energy _____

_____

_____

You at the months end: _____

_____

_____

Take a moment to write down or draw, any feelings, visions or thoughts that have arisen from the cards you pulled for this month.

SEPTEMBER

Week In Advance

Monday — 29

Tuesday — 30

Wednesday — 31

Thursday 1

Friday 2

Saturday 3

Sunday 4

SEPTEMBER

Week In Advance

Monday — 5

Tuesday — 6 ●

Wednesday — 7

Thursday 8

Friday 9

Saturday 10

Sunday 11

SEPTEMBER

New Moon in Virgo

1. How have I prepped my garden
2. The seeds I've sown are growing because of this
3. When I harvest my garden, I will be adding this to my life
4. How can I share my bounty with the world
5. How can I show my garden I am grateful for it

I HAVE NOURISHED MY GARDEN, & NOW I CAN REAP WHAT I SOW. THE FRUITS OF MY LABOUR HAVE CREATED ABUNDANCE IN MY LIFE. I AM BOUNTIFUL, & I AM GRATEFUL

1. HOW HAVE I PREPPED MY GARDEN _____

_____
_____
_____

2. THE SEEDS I'VE SOWN ARE GROWING BECAUSE OF THIS _____

_____
_____
_____

3. WHEN I HARVEST MY GARDEN, I WILL BE ADDING THIS TO MY LIFE

_____
_____
_____

4. HOW CAN I SHARE MY BOUNTY WITH THE WORLD _____

_____
_____
_____

5. HOW CAN I SHOW MY GARDEN I AM GRATEFUL FOR IT _____

_____
_____
_____

SEPTEMBER

Week In Advance

Monday — 12

Tuesday — 13

Wednesday — 14

Thursday 15

Friday 16

Saturday 17

Sunday 18

# SEPTEMBER

Week In Advance

Monday 19

Tuesday 20

Wednesday 21

Thursday 22

Friday 23

Saturday 24

Sunday 25

SEPTEMBER
Full Harvest Moon in Pisces

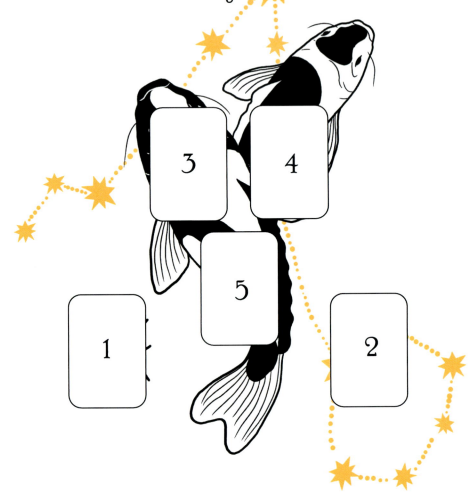

1. What does the full moon trigger in me
2. How do I calm this ocean of emotions
3. When my soul is in waves, how do I ride it out
4. When my soul is calm, how do I appreciate it
5. How do I bring my body and my soul into alignment

I HAVE HONOURED MY BODY & THIS EARTH. NOW, I MUST HONOUR MY SOUL. I CLEANSE MY SPIRIT IN THE LIGHT OF THE MOON & REPLENISH MY BEING. THERE IS AN OCEAN WITHIN ME.

1. WHAT DOES THE FULL MOON TRIGGER IN ME _____
_____
_____
_____

2. HOW DO I CALM THIS OCEAN OF EMOTIONS _____
_____
_____
_____

3. WHEN MY SOUL IS IN WAVES, HOW DO I RIDE IT OUT _____
_____
_____
_____

4. WHEN MY SOUL IS CALM, HOW DO I APPRECIATE IT _____
_____
_____
_____

5. HOW DO I BRING MY BODY AND SOUL INTO ALIGNMENT _____
_____
_____
_____

SEPTEMBER

Week In Advance

Monday — 26

Tuesday — 27

Wednesday — 28 ☽

Thursday 29

Friday 30

Saturday 1

Sunday 2

OCTOBER

SUN	MON	TUE	WED
3	4	5	6
10	11	12	13
17	18	19	20
24	25	26	27
31			

Thu	Fri	Sat
	1	2
7	8	9
14	15	16
21	22	23
28	29	30

New Moon
Libra 13°
Sun & Moon conj. Mars
Sun, Moon, Mars trine Saturn
Mercury trine Jupiter
Mercury square Pluto
Venus sextile Pluto

Full Moon
Aries 27°
Sun conj. Mars
Sun square Pluto
Moon opposte Mars
Moon square Pluto
Mercury trine Saturn
Mercury sextile Venus
Mars trine Jupiter
Mars square Pluto

Last Qtr Moon — Oct 28 Libra
New Moon — Oct 6 Aqua
First Qtr Moon — Oct 12 Taurus
Full Moon — Oct 20 Leo

The Month Ahead

- PERSONAL CHALLENGE
- PERSONAL GROWTH
- YOU AT THE MONTHS START
- YOU AT THE MONTHS END
- EXTERNAL OBSTACLE
- OCTOBER THEME/ENERGY

YOU AT THE MONTHS START: _____

_____

_____

PERSONAL CHALLENGE _____

_____

_____

EXTERNAL OBSTACLE: _____

_____

Personal growth: _____

_____

_____

October's theme/energy _____

_____

_____

You at the months end:_____

_____

_____

Take a moment to write down or draw, any feelings, visions or thoughts that have arisen from the cards you pulled for this month.

OCTOBER

Week In Advance

Monday — 3

Tuesday — 4

Wednesday — 5

Thursday 6

Friday 7

Saturday 8

Sunday 9

OCTOBER
New Moon in Libra

I CREATE HARMONY IN MY LIFE BY EMBRACING THE LIGHT & THE SHADOW. ONE CANNOT EXIST WITHOUT THE OTHER. MY WEAKNESSES ARE THE PLACE WHERE I SHOW MY STRENGTH.

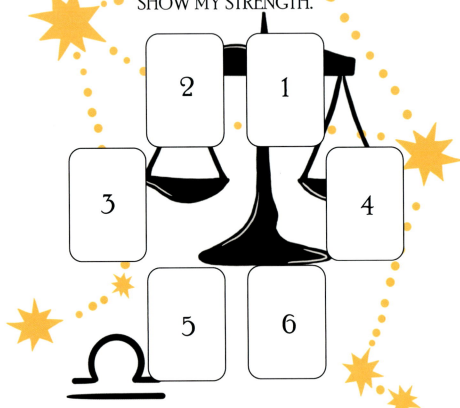

1. WHERE IS THE SHADOW IN MY LIFE
2. WHERE IS THE LIGHT IN MY LIFE
3. WHEN I AM COVERED IN SHADOW, WHERE DOES THE LIGHT GIVE ME HOPE
4. WHEN I AM ILLUMINATED, WHAT SHADOW IS IN MY PERIPHERAL
5. HOW CAN I UNDERSTAND MY SHADOW MORE
6. HOW CAN I BASK IN MY LIGHT MORE

1. WHERE IS THE SHADOW IN MY LIFE _____
_____
_____
_____

2. WHERE IS THE LIGHT IN MY LIFE _____
_____
_____
_____

3. WHEN I AM COVERED IN SHADOW, WHERE DOES THE LIGHT GIVE ME HOPE _____
_____
_____
_____

4. WHEN I AM ILLUMINATED, WHAT SHADOW IS IN MY PERIPHERAL
_____
_____
_____

5. HOW CAN I UNDERSTAND MY SHADOW MORE _____
_____
_____
_____

6. HOW CAN I BASK IN MY LIGHT MORE _____
_____
_____
_____

OCTOBER

Week In Advance

Monday　10

Tuesday　11

Wednesday　12

Thursday 13

Friday 14

Saturday 15

Sunday 16

OCTOBER

Week In Advance

Monday   17

Tuesday   18

Wednesday   19

Thursday 20

Friday 22

Saturday 23

Sunday 24

OCTOBER
Full Blood Moon in Aries

1. How to feed my driving force
2. What is the momentum carrying me
3. My souls fire illuminates what darkness
4. What am I riding away from
5. Where is my unstoppable strength coming from

I HAVE COME SO FAR & STILL HAVE FOUND THE FIRE IN MY SOUL. I AM UNSTOPPABLE, INSURMOUNTABLE & A DRIVING FORVE. THE MOMENTUM I CREATE WILL CARRY ME FORWARD, EVEN IN MY DARKEST HOURS.

1. How to feed my driving force_____
_____
_____
_____

2. What is the momentum carrying me_____
_____
_____
_____

3. My souls fire illuminates what darknesst_____
_____
_____
_____

4. What am I riding away from_____
_____
_____
_____

5. Where is my unstoppable strength coming from_____
_____
_____
_____

OCTOBER

Week In Advance

Monday — 25

Tuesday — 26

Wednesday — 27

Thursday 28

Friday 29

Saturday 30

Sunday 31

NOVEMBER

Sun	Mon	Tue	Wed
	1	2	3
7	8	9	10
14	15	16	17
21	22	23	24
28	29	30	

Thu	Fri	Sat
4 ●	5	6
11	12	13
18	19 ◐ Partial Lunar Eclipse	20
25	26	27 ◑

New Moon
Scorpio 12°
Sun & Moon opposed Uranus
Sun & Moon square Saturn
Mercury square Pluto
Mercury trine Saturn
Mercury sextile Venus
Venus sextile Mars
Mars square Saturn

Full Moon
Libra 8°
Sun conj. Mercury
Sun sextile Pluto
Moon conj. North Node
Moon trine Pluto
Mercury trine Neptune
Mercury opposite Moon
Mars opposite Uranus
Venus sextile Mars
Venus trine Uranus

NOVEMBER

Last Qtr Moon — Nov 27 Libra
New Moon — Nov 4 Aqua
First Qtr Moon — Nov 11 Taurus
Full Moon — Nov 19, Leo

The Month Ahead

- Personal Challenge
- Personal Growth
- You at the Months Start
- You at the Months End
- External Obstacle
- November Theme/Energy

You at the months start: _____

_____

_____

Personal challenge _____

_____

_____

External obstacle: _____

_____

_____

Personal growth: _____
_____
_____

November's theme/energy _____
_____
_____

You at the months end:_____
_____
_____

Take a moment to write down or draw, any feelings, visions or thoughts that have arisen from the cards you pulled for this month.

NOVEMBER

Week In Advance

Monday 1

Tuesday 2

Wednesday 3

Thursday 4

Friday 5

Saturday 6

Sunday 7

NOVEMBER
New Moon in Scorpio

I HAVE DESCENDED DOWN TO THE DEPTHS OF MY OWN INNER HELL TO CONFRONT THE PAIN THAT I HAVE LONG AVOIDED. THERE IS NO ESCAPING WHAT IS REAL, & I HAVE THE POWER TO OVERCOME ANYTHING IN MY WAY. I HAVE TRANSFORMED.

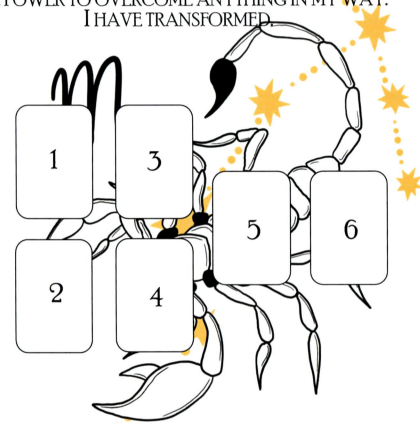

1. WHAT MY DARKEST PARTS ARE TELLING ME
2. HOW AM I HEALING FROM THIS HELLISH PAIN
3. WHEN I OPEN THE DARK DOOR, WHAT DO I SEE
4. HOW WILL I CLIMB OUT OF THIS HELL
5. WHAT IS HEALING WITHIN ME
6. WHAT MY TRANSFORMATION LOOKS LIKE

1. WHAT MY DARKEST PARTS ARE TELLING ME _____
_____
_____
_____

2. HOW AM I HEALING FROM THIS HELLISH PAIN _____
_____
_____
_____

3. WHEN I OPEN THE DOOR, WHAT DO I SEE _____
_____
_____
_____

4. HOW WILL I CLIMB OUT OF THIS HELL _____
_____
_____
_____

5. WHAT IS HEALING WITHIN ME _____
_____
_____
_____

6. WHAT MY TRANSFORMATION LOOKS LIKE _____
_____
_____
_____

NOVEMBER

Week In Advance

Monday — 8

Tuesday — 9

Wednesday — 10

Thursday 11

Friday 12

Saturday 13

Sunday 14

NOVEMBER

Week In Advance

Monday — 15

Tuesday — 16

Wednesday — 17

Thursday 18

Friday 19
PARTIAL LUNAR ECLIPSE

Saturday 20

Sunday 21

NOVEMBER
Full Snow Moon in Taurus

1. When I look at my intentions, what do I see
2. Why would I feel my work is inadequate
3. How to slow down when I work
4. What about my work do I love the most
5. How can I amplify my manifestations

I MANIFEST ALL THAT I WISH TO EXIST. THE INTENTIONS I HAVE PLACED HAVE GIVEN ME A VAST LANDSCAPE OF PROSPERITY & JOY. I SEE THE VALUE IN MY WORK & TAKE TIME TO FIND THE PLEASURE IN ALL THAT I CREATE.

1. WHEN I LOOK AT MY INTENTIONS, WHAT DO I SEE _____
_____
_____
_____

2. WHY WOULD I FEEL MY WORK IS INADEQUATE _____
_____
_____
_____

3. HOW TO SLOW DOWN WHEN I WORK _____
_____
_____
_____

4. WHAT ABOUT MY WORK DO I LOVE THE MOST _____
_____
_____
_____

5. HOW CAN I AMPLIFY MY MANIFESTATIONS _____
_____
_____
_____

NOVEMBER

Week In Advance

Monday 22

Tuesday 23

Wednesday 24

Thursday 25

Friday 26

Saturday 27

Sunday 28

DECEMBER

Sun	Mon	Tue	Wed
			1
5	6	7	8
12	13	14	15
19	20	21	22
26	27	28	29

Thu	Fri	Sat	
2	3	4	**New Moon** Sag 12° Eclipse Sun & Moon conj. Mercury Sun & Moon sextile Saturn Venus conj. Pluto
9	10	11 ● Solar Eclipse	Venus sextile Mars Mars sextile Pluto Mars trine Neptune Mars square Jupiter Saturn square Uranus
16	17 ☽	18	
23	24	25 ○	**Full Moon** Gemini 27° Sun sextile Jupiter Moon trine Jupiter Mercury trine Uranus Venus conj. Pluto Venus sextile Neptune Saturn square Uranus
30	31		

DECEMBER

◐ Last Qtr Moon — Dec 27 Libra
● New Moon — Dec 4 Aqua
◑ First Qtr Moon — Dec 10 Taurus
○ Full Moon — Dec 18, Leo

The Month Ahead

- PERSONAL CHALLENGE
- PERSONAL GROWTH
- YOU AT THE MONTHS START
- YOU AT THE MONTHS END
- EXTERNAL OBSTACLE
- DECEMBER THEME/ENERGY

YOU AT THE MONTHS START: _____

_____

_____

PERSONAL CHALLENGE _____

_____

_____

EXTERNAL OBSTACLE: _____

_____

_____

Personal growth: _____

_____

_____

December's theme/energy _____

_____

_____

You at the months end:_____

_____

_____

Take a moment to write down or draw, any feelings, visions or thoughts that have arisen from the cards you pulled for this month.

December

Week In Advance

Monday · 29

Tuesday · 30

Wednesday · 1

Thursday 2

Friday 3

Saturday 4
SOLAR ECLIPSE

Sunday 5

DECEMBER
New Moon in Sagittarius

1. WHAT IS THE CHAIN HOLDING ME BACK
2. WHAT IS THE WALL MADE OF IN FRONT OF ME
3. WHAT LIMITATIONS HAVE I SET UPON MYSELF
4. WHAT LIMITATIONS HAVE I ALLOWED OTHERS TO SET ON ME
5. MY FUTURE IS CLOSE, HOW DO I GRAB IT

I PUSH PAST THE LIMITATIONS SET UPON ME. THERE IS MORE THAN MEETS THE EYE. I AM UNAFRAID OF WHAT THE FUTURE HOLDS. I SEE THE THRILL OF THE ADBENTURE & LET ME SOUL REACH NEW HEIGHTS.

1. WHAT IS THE CHAIN HOLDING ME BACK_____
_____
_____
_____

2. WHAT IS THE WALL MADE OF IN FRONT OF ME_____
_____
_____
_____

3. WHAT LIMITATIONS HAVE I SET UPON MYSELF_____
_____
_____
_____

4. WHAT LIMITATIONS HAE I ALLOWED OTHERS TO SET ON ME___
_____
_____
_____

5. MT FUTURE IS CLOSE, HOW DO I GRAB IT_____
_____
_____
_____

December

Week In Advance

Monday 6

Tuesday 7

Wednesday 8

Thursday 9

Friday 10

Saturday 11

Sunday 12

DECEMBER

Week In Advance

Monday — 13

Tuesday — 14

Wednesday — 15

Thursday 16

Friday 17

Saturday 18

Sunday 19

DECEMBER
Full Cold Moon in Gemini

1. When I speak, others hear my voice as what
2. How does it feel to speak my truths
3. What part of my soul grows with each honest word
4. What do I see in my own reflection
5. What do others see me as

I HOLD WITHIN ME THE INFINITE WISDOM THAT WEAVES MY SOUL TOGETHER. WHEN I SPEAK FROM THAT PLACE, THE PLACE OF TRUTH, I AM HONOURING MY SPIRIT. I HAVE POWER IN MY VOICE, FOR IT IS A REFLECTION OF MY SOUL

1. WHEN I SPEAK, OTHERS HEAR MY VOICE AS WHAT _____
_____
_____
_____

2. HOW DOES IT FEEL TO SPEAK MY TRUTHS _____
_____
_____
_____

3. WHAT PART OF MY SOUL GROWS WITH EACH HONEST WORD __
_____
_____
_____

4. WHAT DO I SEE IN MY OWN REFLECTION _____
_____
_____
_____

5. WHAT DO OTHERS SEE ME AS _____
_____
_____
_____

DECEMBER

Week In Advance

Monday 20

Tuesday 21

Wednesday 22

Thursday 23

Friday 24

Saturday 25

Sunday 26

December

Week In Advance

Monday — 27

Tuesday — 28

Wednesday — 29

Thursday 30

Friday 31

Saturday 2022 1

Sunday 2022 1

Tarot Key
The Suits

Wands *Your Interpretations*	**Element:** Fire **Key Words:** Drive, Creativity, Ambitious, Goals, Motivation, Vision, Energy, Competition, Passion, Passionate, Restless, Egotism, Pride, Hot-Tempered When a spread is dominated by the **Wands** suit, it indicates that the situation is one that resides mostly in your mind. Something that is weighing on your mind or that you can't stop thinking about.
Cups *Your Interpretations*	**Element:** Water **Key Words:** Emotion, Human Contact, Relationships, Family, Feelings, Desires, Love, Friendship, Connection, Intuition, Sensual Pleasure, Lust Heart-Overruling-Head When a spread is dominated by the **Cups** suit, it indicates that the situation is one that deals with your heart and emotions. Toying with them or something you feel very strongly about.
Swords *Your Interpretations*	**Element:** Air **Key Words:** Intellect, Wisdom, Thought, The Mind, Connection, Expression, Information, Wisdom, Know-It-All, Head Overruling-Heart. When a spread is dominated by the **Swords** suit, it indicates that the situation tends to revolve around change and conflict. This generally does not indicate a harmonious situation, as these are usually ones that cause distress.
Pentacles *Your Interpretations*	**Element:** Earth **Key Words:** Money, Abundance, Substance, Career, Home, Health, Tangible, Reality, Stability, Grounding, Obsession, Possession, Control. When a spread is dominated by the **Pentacles** suit, it indicates that the situation revolves around material aspects, or ones that involve property, home, career, or income.

Tarot Key — Minor Arcana

	Wands	Cups	Swords	Pentacles
Ace	New (creative) idea, birth, fertile time	New relationship, new appreciation for current relationship	Clarity, new understanding, honesty	New job, prosperity, income, starting fresh
Two	Right direction, focused, determined,	Sometimes known as the true lovers card, love, establishing a bond, harmony, understanding	Denial, blocked feelings, being calm but unavailable, unwilling to make a choice	Going with the flow, balancing, dealing with change well, confidence
Three	Rely on yourself, vision the future, support yourself	Friendship, celebration, abundant feelings, community giving, celebrations	Being self aware will bring you a clear head, betrayal, heartbreak, feeling let down	Teamwork, relying on those around you, strategy, obsessed with detail
Four	Completion, celebration, mark the occasion, party	Self-concerned, doubt, questioning, lack of self-appreciation	Retreat, relaxing, staying calm in unknown situations	Limited viewpoint, possessive, feeling its mine
Five	Distress, frustration, competition, challenges, scattered	Disappointment, loss, emotionally confused, emotional resistance	Finding & accepting limitations, hollow victory, defeat, selfish thinking	Worry, loss, illness, victim mentality, rejection, something is missing

	Wands	Cups	Swords	Pentacles
Six	Overcoming adversity, coming out of darkness, victory, pride	Innocence, nostalgia, childhood memories/friends, sentimental, inner child	Leaving the past behind, new perspective, a new positive outlook on life	Bountiful harvest, fruits of your labor, generosity (form you or to you), gifts
Seven	Defensive, confident, saying no, struggling with opposition	Too many options, disorganised, fantasizing the future, high expectations, wishful thinking	Blind to the truth, dishonesty, deception, keeping a secret (from others or yourself)	Evaluating your progress, getting results, planning next moves, taking a small break
Eight	Rushing ahead, movement, developments, swift action	Change of direction, moving on, nothing left in current situation, realizing emotional truths	Feeling trapped, unable to get out without being incredibly hurt, bound, powerless, victim	Honing your craft, mastery, training, discipline and diligence in work, detail oriented
Nine	Vulnerable, cautious, remembering past issues, suspicious, proactively defensive	Wish card, dreams coming true, achieving greatest desires	Guilt, worrying about past transgressions, obsessed with "if only"'s, darkest time before the dawn	Accomplishments, material/financial security, having situational control

Decan = 10 days	Wands	Cups	Swords	Pentacles
Ten	Burden, overextending yourself, workhorse, big workload	Joy, radiating energy, peace, attaining loves ideals, commitment	Rock bottom, being melodramatic, playing the victim, exaggerating self-pity	Experiencing the good things in life, happy family life and home, success
Page	Messenger/messages, childlike exuberance, fresh ideas, take a chance	Youthful energy, young lover, young love, flirtatious, romantic energy	Logical, reasonable, ready for action, wisdom from experience, refreshingly honest	Practical approach, realistic goals, setting plans in motion, new projects
Knight	Daring, passionate, over exaggerates and over promises, adventurous but restless. Last decan of Cancer, first two decans of Leo	Knight in shining armour, emotional rescue, in love with love, many sentiments Last decan of Libra, first two decan of Scorpio	Self-assured, quick action, charging ahead, impatient, cut off from emotion Last decan of Capricorn, first two decans of Aquarius	Hardworking, responsible, passionless effort, working for the sake of working Last decan of Aries, first two decans of Taurus
Queen	Know what you want & where you're going, attractive, magnetic, leader, optimistic. Last decan of Pisces, first two decans of Aries	Prioritizing emotional understanding, unconditional love, empathy, emotional involvement, Last decan of Gemini, first two decans of Cancer	Problem solving, up-front and honest, realistic plans, judgemental, fast thinker. Last decan of Virgo, first two decans of Libra	Reliability, loyal, home-loving, lover of animals & children, resourceful. Last decan of Sagittarius, first two decans of Capricorn
King	Bold, dramatic, inspiring, leader, art mastery, charismatic, male authority figure. Last decan of Scorpio, first two decans of Sagittarius	Emotional maturity and security, keeping emotionally calm, balancing atmosphere. Last decan of Aquarius, first two decans of Pisces	Direct, assertive, objective outlook, cutting through mental confusion. Last decan of Taurus, first two decans of Gemini	Enterprises, made it to the top, responsible, practical, stabilizing. Last decan of Leo, first two decans of Virgo

Tarot Key

The Fool (0) *Uranus*	Impulsive, childlike, jumping in, spontaneous, new beginnings,	
The Magician (1) *Mercury*	All of the tools to achieve, goal focused, knowledge.	
The High Priestess (2) *Moon*	Secrets (revealed), seeing beyond what's in front of you, the unknown.	
The Empress (3) *Venus*	Action, development, harmony with the natural world, creative	
The Emperor (4) *Aries*	Power, authority figure, leadership, structure thought	
The Hierophant (5) *Taurus*	Teacher, teaching, knowledge seeker,	
The Lovers (6) *Gemini*	What is love, relationships of all kinds, union, commitment	
The Chariot (7) *Cancer*	Diligence, willpower, things happening at fast pace	
Strength (8) *Leo*	Courage, inner strength, self-awareness	
The Hermit (9) *Virgo*	Withdrawing, spending time alone, self-searching	
Wheel of Fortune (10) *Jupiter*	Fate, inevitability, destiny, timing, change is coming	

Major Arcana

Justice (11) *Libra*	Fairness, balancing, accepting the truth	
The Hanged Man (12) *Neptune*	Being in limbo, paradox, being at a crossroads, taking a step back	
Death (13) *Scorpio*	New beginnings, change, transformation	
Temperance (14) *Sagittarius*	Self-control, harmony, understanding, balancing opposing factors	
The Devil (15) *Capricorn*	Obsession, materialism, temptation, addiction, negative thoughts	
The Tower (16) *Mars*	Disruption, sudden unexpected change, unwelcomed change, chaos	
The Star (17) *Aquarius*	Self-expression, visionary progress, inspiration, seeing the light in the dark	
The Moon (18) *Pisces*	Intuition, shadow self, worried, apprehensive, blind to the truth	
The Sun (19) *Sun*	Shining down, happiness, warmth in your soul, sharing joy	
Judgement (20) *Pluto*	Forgiveness (of others & the self,) acceptance, taking account, no blame	
The World (21) *Saturn*	Completion, fulfilment, achievement, happiness, accomplishment, acceptance	

Zodiacs

Before we get into the correspondences around each Zodiac season, I want to point out a few things when it comes to the dates and timing of each one. There is no "one and done" timeframe for the Zodiac signs. Due to the extra 25% of a day we get each year, and the whole extra day on Leap Years, the start and end times of each season can differ by a day or two, year to year. As well, the sun does not move on a calendar or change signs at midnight, so 99.9% of the time, the signs will end and start on the same day as the sign previous to them.

This means that if you were born really early on the last day of Libra, and someone else was born late on the first day of Scorpio, it is possible you will have the same birth *date* but different sun signs. Your birth *time,* and your birth *location* are only part of the requirements for figuring out your accurate sun sign, especially if your birth date is at the end or beginning of a zodiac season.

Simple googling "sun times for entering zodiacs for (your location)" will give you an accurate timeframe year to year. The dates below include several of the variations of dates for each sign.

Aries Mar 21/24 - Apr 18/21 	**Element:** Fire. **Status:** Cardinal. **Day:** Tuesday. **Planet:** Mars, Sun. **Colours:** Scarlett, White, Pink. **Chakras:** Root, Solar Plexus, Brow. **Seasons:** Spring, Summer. **Celebration:** Spring Equinox **Crystals:** Bloodstone, Diamond, Ruby, Red Jasper, Garnet. **Herbs:** Geranium, Sage, Tiger Lily, Thistle, Rose. **Deities:** Isis, Athena, Shiva, Mars, Minerva. **Tarot:** The Emperor. **Intentions & Powerflow:** Ambition, Beginnings, Courage, Desires, Growth, Leadership, Lust, Needs, Obstacles, Passion, Pregnancy, Sexuality, Warmth
Taurus Apr 21/23 - May 20/24 	**Element:** Earth. **Status:** Fixed **Day:** Friday **Planet:** Earth, Venus **Colours:** Red, Orange, Brown, Indigo **Chakras:** Root, Heart, Throat **Season:** Spring **Crystals:** Sapphire, Turquoise, Jade, Emerald, Topaz. **Herbs:** Burdock, Elder, Vervain, Violet, Wild Rose, Clover. **Deities:** Osiris, Apis, Asar, Hera, Venus **Tarot:** The Empress, The Hierophant, Pentacles **Intentions & Powerflow:** Affection, Comfort, Dedication, Endurance, Grounding, Intuition, Life, Love, Lust, the Mind, Money, Organize, Patience, Protection, the Sense, Stability, Wealth

Gemini May 22/26- June 18-21 	**Element:** Air. **Status:** Mutable. **Day:** Wednesday **Planet:** Mercury, Uranus. **Colours:** White, Yellow, Orange. **Chakras:** Heart, Throat. **Season:** Summer **Crystals:** Moss Agate, Onyx, Jade, Topaz, Diamond. **Herbs:** Orchid, Dill, Gladioli, Parsley, Iris, Snapdragon. **Deities:** Bast & Sekhmet, Castor & Pollux, Frey & Freyja, Janus. **Tarot:** The Magician, The Lovers **Intentions & Powerflow:** Adaptability, Balance, Change, Communication, Creativity, Emotions, Intelligence, Knowledge, Relationships, Truth
Cancer June 19/22- July 20/23 	**Element:** Water. **Status:** Cardinal. **Day:** Monday. **Planet:** Moon, Pluto, Sun **Colours:** Amber, White, Silver **Chakras:** Sacral, Solar Plexus, Heart. **Season:** Summer. **Celebration:** Midsummer's Eve. **Crystals:** Moonstone, Cats Eye, Pearl, Emerald, Amber. **Herbs:** Passion Flower, Balm, Comfrey, Water Lily. **Deities:** Khapera, Mercury, Apollo. **Tarot:** The High Priestess, The Chariot **Intentions & Powerflow:** Beginnings, Change, Connections, Conscious & Sub Consciousness, Emotions, Family, the Home, Imagination, Intuition, Love, Magic, Nurture, Protection, Psychic Ability, Romance, Shyness, Support, Sympathy
Leo July 22/24- Aug 21-23 	**Element:** Fire. **Status:** Fixed. **Day:** Sunday. **Planet:** Sun **Colours:** Amber, White, Silver **Chakras:** Solar Plexus, Heart. **Season:** Summer. **Crystals:** Amber, Ruby, Diamond, Golden Topaz. **Herbs:** Chamomile, Saffron, Sunflower, Marigold **Deities:** Horus, Sekhmet, Demeter, Vishnu, Venus **Tarot:** Strength, The Sun, Wands **Intentions & Powerflow:** Action, Affection, Ambition, Communication, Confidence, Courage, Determination, Friendship, Growth, Guardian, Guidance, Leadership, Light, Love, Loyalty, Animal Magic, Passion, Pleasure, Pride, Romance, Strength, Warmth, Willpower
Virgo Aug 22-24- Sept 20-22	**Element:** Earth **Status:** Mutable **Day:** Wednesday **Planet:** Earth, Mercury. **Colours:** Moss Green, Mauve, Rose, Pink **Chakras:** Sacral, Solar Plexus, Throat **Season:** Summer. **Crystals:** Jade, Carnelian, Diamond, Jasper, Aquamarine, Peridot **Herbs:** Lily, Narcissus, Rosemary, Snowdrop, Silver Root **Deities:** Hera, Isis, Adonis, Ceres **Tarot:** The Magician, The Hermit **Intentions & Powerflow:** Abundance, Beginnings, Cycles, Destiny, Endings, Grounding, Independence, Intuition, Love, Organize, Purification, Success, Well-Being

Libra Sept 21/23- Oct 20/22	**Element:** Air. **Status:** Cardinal **Day:** Friday **Planet:** Saturn, Venus, **Colours:** Emerald Green Royal Blue, Black **Chakras:** Sacral, Heart **Season:** Autumn **Crystals:** Lapis Lazuli, Jade, Opal, Emerald. **Herbs:** Violet, Yarrow, White Rose. **Deities:** Maat, Ma, Themis, Yama, Vulcan. **Tarot:** Justice, Empress **Intentions & Powerflow:** Attract, Balance, Business, Community, Cooperation, Fairness, Grace, Harmony, Justice, Love, Romance, Sensitivity, Sympathy, Unity
Scorpio Oct 21/23- Nov 19/21 	**Element:** Water. **Status:** Fixed. **Day:** Tuesday. **Planet:** Mars, Pluto **Colours:** Black, Blue, Purple, Crimson **Chakras:** Root, Sacral. **Season:** Autumn. **Crystals:** Aquamarine, Ruby, Topaz, Jet. **Herbs:** Chrysanthemum, Pine, Rosemary, Vanilla **Deities:** Hecate, Hel, Isis, Persephone, Anubis, Mars, Pluto. **Tarot:** Death, Swords **Intentions & Powerflow:** Authority, Change, Clairvoyance, Control, Darkness, Death, Desire, Emotions, Energy, Healing, Jealousy, Loyalty, Lust, the Underworld, Passion, Power, Psychic Ability, Rebirth, Revenge, Spirituality, Trust, Willpower.
Sag. Nov 20/22- Dec 19/21	**Element:** Fire. **Status:** Mutable **Day:** Thursday. **Planet:** Jupiter **Colours:** Red, Crimson, Darker Shades **Chakras:** Root, Solar Plexus, Brow. **Season:** Autumn **Celebration:** Winter Solstice **Crystals:** Sapphire, Amethyst, Diamond, Golden Topaz. **Herbs:** Carnation, Pink Clover, Rush, Sage, Wildflower **Deities:** Nepthys, Apollo, Artemis, Vishnu, Diana **Tarot:** Temperance, Wheel of Fortune **Intentions & Powerflow:** Beauty, Consciousness, Dream Work, Enlightenment, Fear, Freedom, Growth, Honesty, Independence, Intuition, Knowledge, Magic, Prophecy, Self-Work, Sexuality, Travel, Truth, Unity
Capr. Dec 20/23- Jan 18/20 	**Element:** Earth **Status:** Cardinal **Day:** Thursday **Planet:** Earth, Saturn **Colour:** Gray, Dark, Brown, Indigo, Black **Celebration:** Winter Solstice: **Chakras:** Root, Crown **Season:** Winter **Crystals:** Malachite, Onyx, Garnet, Jet, Obsidian, Turquoise. **Herbs:** Belladonna, Hellebore, Rue, Hemlock, Orris Root **Deities:** Set, Pan, Hermes, Vesta, Bacchus. **Tarot:** The Devil **Intentions & Powerflow:** Accomplishment, Ambition, Beginnings, Confidence, Focus, Cycles, Darkness, Death, Determination, Endings, Grounding, Intuition, Love, Manifestation, Omens, Negativity, Obstacles, Patience, Psychic Ability, Responsibility, Stability, Success, Willpower.

Aquar. Jan 19/21- Feb 16/18 	**Element:** Air. **Status:** Fixed **Day:** Saturday **Planet:** Uranus, Neptune, Saturn **Colours:** Violet, Purple, Sky Blue **Chakras:** Throat, Brow, Crown. **Season:** Winter **Celebration:** Imbolc **Crystals:** Garnet, Amber, Aquamarine, Lapis Lazuli, Malachite **Herbs:** Buttercup, Fennel, Wormwood **Deities:** Nuit, Athena, Juno, Isis, Ea **Tarot:** The Fool, The Star, Cups **Intentions & Powerflow:** Ambition, Charity, Community Compassion, Creativity, Determination, Freedom, Friendship, Healing, Honesty, Integrity, Intuition, Loyalty, Peace, Spirituality, Wisdom
Pisces Feb 18/20- Mar 19/21 	**Element:** Water **Status:** Mutable **Day:** Thursday. **Planet:** Neptune, Jupiter. **Colours:** Purple, Crimson, Aqua, Lavender **Chakras:** Brow, Crown. **Season:** Winter **Celebration:** Spring Equinox **Crystals:** Amethyst, Pearl, Sapphire, Emerald **Herbs:** Heliotrope, Carnation, Poppy, Sage **Deities:** Anubis, Khepera, Poseidon, Vishnu, Neptune **Tarot:** The Hanged Man, The Moon **Intentions & Powerflow:** Adaptability, Boundaries, Calm, Clarity, Communication, Compassion, Creativity, Death, Emotions, Enchantment, Imagination, Intuition, Justice, Kindness, Psychic Ability, Romance, Sensitivity, Spirituality, Unity.

Made in the USA
Middletown, DE
02 February 2021